Begin Again

Utilize the Wisdom of Eastern and
Western Ideologies to Achieve Your
Full Potential

Brian C. Hite, Ph.D.

ISBN (paperback) - 979-8-88759-113-1
ISBN (eBook) -979-8-88759-114-8

Free Bonus Content

To say thanks for buying my book, I would like to give you the first 15 essays of my next book for FREE!

www.beginagainperformancepsychology.com/bonuscontent

Dedication

To my precious Firebird…the Phoenix in my life who, with her boundless energy, insatiable curiosity, perpetual optimism, bottomless compassion, massive heart, and unquenchable thirst for new experiences, reminds me constantly to Begin Again.

Table of Contents

Introduction

"To vanquish sin, you must accept that the root of each sin is in a bad thought. We are only the consequences of what we think." Buddha

"The happiness of your life depends on the quality of your thoughts." Marcus Aurelius

"Too many people are unaware that it is not outer events or circumstances that will create happiness; rather, it is our perception of events and of ourselves that will create, or uncreate, positive emotions." Albert Ellis

The three quotes above illustrate the essence of this book for two reasons. First, each quote describes a fundamental attribute of human nature that has been recognized for thousands of years: what we call "reality" is unique to and created by each of us. What we call "reality" is our interpretations of and explanations for what happens to and around us. From this perspective, the extent to which something is good or bad, right or wrong, important or trivial, depends entirely on how we choose to think about it.

Second, these words were written by people who lived at different times and in different places around the globe. Each of these individuals faced markedly different sets of challenges and circumstances and had different goals and objectives in mind when they recorded their insights. However, as unique as each thinker's situation was, each came to almost identical conclusions about this critical component of human experience.

Structure

This book contains 183 short essays on topics gleaned from various sources spanning both miles and millennia. Each essay highlights a familiar challenge, discusses that challenge through the lens of wisdom put forth by a wide variety of thinkers, and offers practical ways to apply that wisdom in daily life.

The concepts presented don't come from a single source. Rather they find support across philosophical, religious, spiritual, or scientific traditions throughout time and across cultures. Take, for example, the concept of "impermanence".

- In the East, impermanence was written about in the Pali Canon, one of the earliest Buddhist writings, and critical Hindu texts such as the Bhagavad Gita and the Principle Upanishads.

- In the West, the early Greek philosopher Heraclitus (famous for "No man ever steps in the same river twice") introduced the concept of impermanence when he distinguished "becoming" from "being".

- In modern times, physicists have accepted the truth of entropy (i.e., the tendency for matter to naturally and continuously move from a state of order to disorder); while neuroscientists, beginning in the early 1900s, have produced reams of research detailing the way our brains constantly restructure themselves throughout our lives…a concept known as neuroplasticity.

Neither the number nor order of essays is random. Including exactly 183 essays allows the reader to engage with a new concept every other day over the course of one year. Why every other day? Because learning and behavioral change require regular, consistent practice. An emphasis on practice can be found in the writings of Eastern thinkers going back to the Bhagavad Gita and early Buddhist texts, Western thinkers such as Aristotle and Herodotus, and modern scientists publishing and presenting on issues such as "deliberate practice".

In line with these recommendations for practice, the reader is encouraged to read each essay and intentionally practice its suggestions for action on two consecutive days. This repetition will help lock in knowledge, increase awareness of the concepts during daily life, and provide a kickstart to new, more productive behaviors.

Like the number, the order of essays was also deliberately chosen. Each concept appears several times, but in different forms and contexts, throughout the book. This structure is, again, designed to maximize retention by providing periodic reminders that reinforce earlier learning and solidify the concepts and suggestions more firmly in the reader's mind.

The Future

Finally, this book was designed to be read repeatedly, year after year. None of us are the same from one year to the next, and the hope is that freshly engaging with this book each year will provide at least two benefits. First, rereading the material will increase readers' depth of knowledge and remind them of the daily actions they can take to foster well-being. Second, because we all change from year to year, information that didn't resonate or wasn't relevant in past years might be highly relevant and resonate very strongly this year.

My sincerest hope is that readers relate to the challenges

common to each of us, learn and grow from the wisdom put forth by many incredible thinkers throughout the ages, and experience real-world benefits from applying the concrete suggestions in their everyday lives.

Begin Again

Every day we begin again. Every day is an opportunity for growth, development, change, and improvement. Every moment is a chance to assess our current circumstances and steer our thoughts and actions in more helpful, productive directions. There are three requirements, however, for these positive changes to occur: self-awareness, acceptance, and the ability to self-regulate.

Without awareness of what we are thinking, feeling, and doing, we are like pinballs bouncing through the machine of life. Instead of proactively influencing our environments, we reactively respond to whatever we encounter. Our life's direction is not freely chosen but determined by random quirks built into the pinball machine in which we exist.

To avoid this haphazard, chaotic existence, we must cultivate self-awareness. We have to develop the ability to tune in to the types of thoughts we have and the specific emotions they drive. We must enhance our ability to recognize not only our choices and behaviors but the consequences of our actions…for ourselves and those around us.

Once we are aware of our thoughts, emotions, and actions, we must accept them exactly as they are. This doesn't mean that we acquiesce to our circumstances and resign ourselves to living in our current state forever. It means that we accept reality as it is without exaggerating, glossing over, or ignoring any aspect of our experiences. Only with this acceptance can we identify the best paths to positive change.

Finally, after becoming aware of and accepting our present experiences, we need to self-regulate. We must manipulate our thoughts, emotions, and behaviors in ways that facilitate the change we would like to see occur. We shift our thinking in more productive directions; learn to lean into and harness our emotions for stronger relationships and better performance; and engage in behavior that maximizes health, productivity, and overall well-being.

Although self-awareness, acceptance, and self-regulation are necessary for us to flourish, we often fall short in one or all of these areas…and that's okay. When that inevitability occurs, we just need to Begin Again.

When we recognize that our thinking is heading down counterproductive roads, our emotions are overwhelming or counterproductive, or our actions are harmful for ourselves or others, we simply need to stop, reset, and start over. We Begin Again by adopting more adaptive thinking styles, exploring and accepting our emotions, and implementing behaviors aligned with our values and goals.

Similarly, if your attempts to implement the strategies in this book don't yield stellar results the first time around, Begin Again. If you find yourself in some of the circumstances described in these essays and fall back on well-established but counterproductive habits rather than employing the more helpful and productive suggestions you've read, Begin Again.

Reality exists only in the Here and Now. So, right now…no matter what has happened in the past…you have the freedom to Begin Again.

1

Embrace Challenge

*"No tree becomes rooted and sturdy unless many a wind assails it. For
by its very tossing it tightens its grip and plants its roots more securely;
the fragile trees are those that have grown in a sunny valley."*
– Seneca

Challenges in life are both inevitable and necessary.
Although difficulties we face daily can be daunting at
times, these very difficulties allow us to grow and develop
as individuals. These adversities force us to delve deeply within
ourselves, to lean on and pull from various resources. Each time
we use these resources, just like each time we use a muscle, that
resource becomes more robust and better able to help us the next
time we find ourselves in need of its benefits.

So, the next time you encounter a challenge or difficulty, ask
yourself how you might improve as a result of experiencing this
challenge. See if you can transform frustration into gratitude.
That is, try to change your perception from one of being thwarted
or hindered in some way to one of being afforded a unique
opportunity to improve, develop, and grow.

Problems and challenges will arise in our lives no matter what,
and thank goodness! Imagine how boring life would be and how

stagnant we would become without occasional opportunities to flex our "resilience muscles". Today, choose to embrace those challenges you encounter and be thankful for the chance to get a little better today than you were yesterday.

2

Everything Went Wrong...or Did It?

"You may encounter many defeats, but you must not be defeated. In fact, it may be necessary to encounter the defeats, so you can know who you are, what you can rise from, how you can still come out of it."
– Maya Angelou
"Failure is success if we learn from it." – Malcolm Forbes

How do you handle situations when things don't go as planned? Some people see these situations as learning opportunities, while others view them as evidence of a personal defect. When considering why things didn't go the way we'd hoped, some people heap all blame and responsibility for the situation on themselves. Others place all responsibility and blame for things going awry on random circumstances or other people.

When our actions don't result in the outcomes we would like, how we explain those results will affect our confidence, motivation, energy levels, attention, relationships, and overall well-being... not to mention our future actions and the likelihood of things working out better the next time around.

The next time something doesn't go how you wanted it to, notice how you think about and handle that situation. Do you see the aberration as an opportunity for learning and development or as a failure that has knocked you down and set you back in irrevocable ways? Also, notice the reasons you give for why things didn't go as planned. Are those reasons fixated solely on your own role? Do those reasons implicate others and absolve you completely? Or, is there a fair and honest balance between your role and the roles others or circumstances played?

Things aren't always going to work out the way we want them to. When they don't, perceiving the situation as an opportunity for growth and evaluating the causes in a thorough, honest, and unbiased manner can help us maintain our confidence and motivation, sustain and improve relationships with others, and maximize the likelihood that we will be more effective in the future.

3

Confidence

"Once we believe in ourselves, we can risk curiosity, wonder,
spontaneous delight, or any experience that reveals the human spirit."
—e. e. cummings

As much as we'd like to be able to approach every endeavor with confidence, the reality is that sometimes we have doubts about our ability to do what we'd like to do successfully. In those moments, rather than submitting to our uncertainty about our capabilities, I encourage you to try boosting your confidence by asking and answering four questions.

First, *Have you done this thing before, and if so, how did it turn out?* If you've done this thing before and succeeded, you can think back to that situation and remember the effort, strategies, and attitude you used to succeed. If you failed the last time, think about why you failed. Identify those things you might do differently that can help you succeed this time around.

Second, *If you haven't done this specific thing before, have you done something that requires similar abilities?* Maybe you haven't done this exact thing before, but if you've done something that requires similar skills, energy levels, or mindsets, you can think back on successful encounters with those other tasks to build confidence for the task at hand.

Third, *Have you seen anybody else do this thing before? Or can you watch somebody do this thing sometime soon?* When we watch somebody else do something, particularly people who are similar to us, we can gain confidence by identifying what these people did that led to success or what they didn't do that led to failure. With this knowledge, we can engage in the activity or task with much more confidence because we know what to do or avoid that will maximize the likelihood that we'll be successful.

Fourth, *What are others saying to you about your ability to succeed? What are you saying to yourself about your ability to succeed?* When we receive encouragement from others we respect, trust, and admire, our confidence can rise tremendously. Similarly, we can encourage ourselves and boost our confidence by engaging in affirming self-talk (e.g., You can do it; You've done this before; You've overcome more demanding challenges than this). We can also focus on aspects of the situation that we can control (e.g., attitude, strategies, effort) and choose to perceive our situation as a challenge and an opportunity for growth and improvement.

Confidence not only feels great to have but makes it more likely that we will be at our best in any given circumstance. However, constantly having high levels of confidence is impossible. Doubt and uncertainty in some situations are simply a part of life. When that doubt creeps into your mind, keep in mind the four questions above. If you ask, answer, and act based on the answers to those four questions, you should notice a significant boost in your confidence.

4

Challenging Conversations

"If you think that it is necessary to judge your neighbor, then say this looking directly into his eyes, and say this in such a way that you do not create animosity." – Tolstoy

When challenging conversations with people we care about need to happen, ensuring that the conversation includes all six of these components will help increase the likelihood that the issue you're addressing is solved and that your relationship will remain strong.

First, make sure you're clear in your own mind what, exactly, the problem is you're trying to address. Also, think about any factors that might hinder (e.g., fatigue, strong emotion) or help (e.g., patience, breathing, tone of voice) you communicate effectively.

Second, lay out the problem for the other person as clearly and succinctly as possible. Tell the other person in as objective and specific terms as possible what the issue is as you see it.

Third, tell the other person why this issue matters to you, why you care, why this problem is important to you.

Fourth, ask the other person if they also think there's a problem. If so, do they see the problem the same way you do? This is important because developing any sort of solution is impossible if both people don't agree on the problem to be solved.

Fifth, ask the other person what the two of you can do to alleviate the issue. What steps can the two of you agree on and commit to that are likely to eliminate the problem you both agree exists?

Lastly, explicitly lay out the goodness the two of you can expect once the issue has been resolved. You might also tell them about the badness you both can expect if the issue is NOT resolved. The point is that the natural ramifications of the problem being resolved (or not) need to be clearly communicated.

By ensuring that your conversation contains these six parts, you can maximize the likelihood of resolving challenging issues that need to be addressed with people you care about. However, even if the problem is not resolved, approaching the discussion this way will make it more likely that your relationship will remain strong, so the door to future conversations will remain open. So, if necessary, you can try again later.

5

Connection

"We must, indeed, all hang together or, most assuredly, we shall all hang separately." -Benjamin Franklin

C onnections with others are essential for us to not be at our best but to live in a world at its best.

Relationships with others are tremendous resources that come with an assortment of support. This might be emotional support, physical support, psychological support, spiritual support, or financial support. Regardless of the type of support we get from others, it's support that helps us function to our potential and be at our best during challenging moments in our lives.

Providing support to others can build resources as well. When others need support, supplying help that makes them stronger makes us stronger, too. So, by taking the time to understand what someone else needs and addressing those needs in a meaningful way, both you and the person you're helping grow and become better together.

Although giving support to and receiving support from individuals is undoubtedly helpful, we can also connect and develop relationships with larger entities like our families or organizations. Taking the time to host and attend family gatherings and offering your abilities and strengths to organizations you believe in or are a part of can create a strong sense of connection that benefits both you and the group you've chosen to connect with.

So, at both the individual and group levels, connections we develop can help all parties...ourselves, others, and even organizations, function as well as possible. And when enough of these connections are made and sustained in our society, and both people and organizations are at their best, the world becomes a much more friendly, inviting, engaging, and supportive place to live.

6

Acceptance

"You accept things as they are, not as you wish they were in this moment. This is important to understand. You can wish for things in the future to be different, but in this moment you have to accept things as they are." – Deepak Chopra

Before making any changes or improvements in our lives, we first have to accept reality as it currently is. Acceptance seems counterintuitive to some people because they think acceptance is synonymous with acquiescence or passivity. However, acceptance is not the act of submitting to things as they are and giving up any pursuit of betterment. Acceptance is simply the acknowledgment of our current circumstances, an honest appraisal of reality as it currently exists. And without this honest appraisal, it is impossible to take any sort of action to improve our situation.

For example, if my relationship with my teenager is currently on rocky ground, I must accept this fact before I can take any steps to strengthen that relationship. Suppose I try to talk myself into believing that the relationship is fine instead of accepting that my relationship with my child is currently in a bad place. In that case, I won't take any steps to improve the relationship. Why would I? Because I haven't accepted the reality of the damaged relationship, I won't believe there is anything to improve…so I will make no effort to improve it.

Although accepting our current situations is critical to progress, accurate assessments of our circumstances can be challenging. As in the relationship example above, there might be considerable pain associated with honestly acknowledging the challenges we face. So, instead, we rationalize or ignore those challenges altogether. We might also be so focused on other things, things we've deemed more important than the challenging situation, that we don't recognize how bad things have actually gotten.

To help ensure that we have an accurate picture of our current reality, we need to take the time to assess honestly what is going on around us and within us. We need to question our initial perceptions of situations we encounter by asking ourselves how else the situation might be perceived. Also, before having a conversation with someone about something important, we need to take time to think about and truly understand the situation from both our and the other person's perspectives. In this way, we can address the causes of the problem rather than the symptoms.

So, as you go through your day, I encourage you to take some time now and then to check in with your current circumstances. What is going on around you? What thoughts are in your mind? What emotions are you experiencing? What is your body's internal state (e.g., muscle tension, rapid breathing)? Whatever you encounter, whatever the answers you come up with, accept those answers…accept your reality. Once you have…and ONLY once you have…progress is possible.

7

Dare to Demonstrate Integrity

"Live in such a way that you would not be ashamed to sell your pet parrot to the town gossip." – Will Rogers

How often do we succumb to the pressure to portray ourselves in a way that is not authentic? How often do we choose to dress or act in a certain way, attend certain events, or engage with certain people solely to avoid feeling separated or different from those around us? How often do we behave in ways we know we shouldn't because we fear how other people will respond if we do what we believe to be right?

These fears are normal and natural. However, giving in to these fears can have horrible consequences for ourselves, our kids, and our relationships with others.

First, when we say one thing and do another, other people notice. They recognize our hypocrisy and lose both respect and trust. People admire individuals whose actions match their words, who live the way they advise others to live. This goes for friends, colleagues, children, and subordinates at work. Regardless of the nature of your relationship with someone, that relationship will deteriorate every time you behave in ways you've explicitly criticized and strengthen every time your behaviors align with ones you've publicly endorsed.

Second, when we say one thing and do another, we notice. When our behaviors don't align with what we think we should do, we experience an uncomfortable feeling called cognitive dissonance that can only be resolved in one of two ways: 1) Changing our ideas about how we ought to behave or 2) Justifying how we did behave.

Self-justification is something that comes all too naturally to us and often occurs without our even being aware of it. We snap at someone and justify it by saying that we are just tired or hungry. We're late to an event and justify it by emphasizing how busy we are. We give a bad presentation at work and justify it by blaming the boss for not giving us the time, resources, guidance, etc., that we needed to be successful.

This justification reduces cognitive dissonance but does nothing to help us improve as individuals. In our minds, we have nothing to improve because outside circumstances beyond our control were responsible for why we did not act the way we believe we should.

Today, consider three of your most deeply held values/ morals. Maybe timeliness, patience, commitment, persistence, compassion, or hard work. Whatever your values/morals, pay special attention to how the words and actions you choose today align with those values/morals. Chances are, some of your actions and words will align, and some won't. Either way, tune into the feelings you have in those moments and how you handled those feelings. For example, if compassion was a value you chose and you demonstrated compassion by giving a homeless person some money, how did you feel? Alternatively, if compassion was a value you chose but you passed a homeless person on the street without even a glance in their direction, how did you feel? Finally, what was the story you told yourself about your behavior? Did you justify behavior that was not aligned with your values?

The more we behave as we believe in our core that we ought to, the stronger our relationships will be, the more personal growth and development become possible, and the more peace and overall well-being we'll experience.

8

Why Are Goals Good?

"The human soul dishonors itself...when it fails to direct any of its actions or impulses toward a goal, but instead acts without purpose and without attention..." – Marcus Aurelius

Most of us set goals regularly. We might set small goals (e.g., finishing the laundry) or large goals (e.g., starting a business). Regardless of what kind of goals we set, there are benefits associated with having an objective in mind that we can regularly pursue.

Goals define the desired end state. Instead of simply reacting to whatever life throws at us, goals allow us to be proactive by giving us a precise target we can shoot for, something unambiguous we can direct our attention and efforts toward. As a result, having a specific goal to focus on helps reduce the likelihood that we will succumb to the inevitable distractors that assail us regularly throughout our day.

Goals provide us an easy way to assess progress. Too often, we find ourselves wondering if our efforts are making any real difference in our lives or the lives of those we care about. Goals, however, provide us with a concrete way to track our growth and development on a regular and objective basis.

Goals remind us of our larger purpose. That sense of purpose motivates us and keeps us driving forward in productive directions despite life's inevitable challenges.

So, throughout your day today, keep your goals in the forefront of your mind. You can do this with sticky notes, a whiteboard, a desk calendar, strategically placed pictures, or your preferred technological gadget. Whatever your tactic, choose one and use it regularly. Also, in addition to keeping the goal itself top of mind, keep the reason why you are pursuing that goal top of mind. Always remember why the goal is important to you. Those two strategies will minimize distraction and maximize the likelihood that you'll make regular progress toward your goals.

9

What's Your Opinion?

How do you decide what's true? When presented with new information, how do you form an opinion? How do you decide whether to believe what you're hearing or not?

When we hear new information, we often experience an immediate emotional reaction. Then, based on that emotional reaction, we determine whether we believe the information or not. That is, our opinion about a matter tends not to be based on a thorough analysis of the relevant facts but solely on how the information makes us feel.

When our opinions are grounded not in fact but in emotion, it is very easy for us to make mistakes, jump to conclusions, and act in impulsive ways we are likely to regret later.

The next time you are presented with new information, take a moment to tune into your immediate feelings about that information. What emotions did that information elicit in you?

Then, notice the temptation to accept the truth of the information and act on the information in ways determined by your emotions. Finally, take the time to dig a little more deeply into the information itself. Take the time to evaluate the information rationally and thoroughly.

In this way, we can avoid being sucked into believing false information simply as a result of manipulative presentation, persuasive marketing, or cognitive biases. We can be more confident that our opinions and beliefs are grounded in logic, rationality, and fact.

10

Goals – The Why

"What you get by achieving your goals is not as important as what you become by achieving your goals." – Henry David Thoreau

Long-term goals are challenging to achieve for several reasons:

1. They require sustained effort over long periods of time.
2. They require you to balance many different components of life to maintain that sustained effort for as long as necessary.
3. Life's inevitable challenges will require you to change the plans you've created and put into action.
4. Due to fatigue, boredom, or other unforeseen circumstances, motivation to achieve the goal will wain over time.

The challenges listed are very likely to occur, and any one of these challenges can derail an individual's goal pursuit very quickly. One strategy, though, can help combat all the challenges listed in a strong, predictable, and thorough manner. That is, understand your "Why" and remind yourself of this "Why" every chance you get.

Why did you set this goal? Why do you care about achieving

this goal? Why does achieving this goal matter to you? Why is achieving this goal so important? The answers to these questions constitute your "Why" and can serve as a shield against the blows incurred by the challenges listed above. Not all answers to these questions are created equally, though. Not all answers to these questions will avert the challenges above.

For example, if the answers you come up with are in the vein of, "To get a reward," "So people will like me and think I'm important," "To avoid feeling guilty or ashamed," or "To be seen as better than somebody else," you are setting yourself up for failure. Although these "Why's" can be motivating in short, situational contexts, they tend not to be motivating over time. When challenges arise, we tend to care less about the reward, decide that we don't really care what other people think, or come up with excuses for why not achieving the goal is reasonable and rational.

On the other hand, if the answers you come up with connect the goal to your values, you are much more likely to persevere when life's curveballs are thrown at you. For example, if one of your values is family, your "Why" might be something like, "Because achieving this goal will provide stability and security for my family" or "Pursuing and achieving this goal allows me to model the right behavior for my kids." These are "Why's" that will, no matter how daunting the challenge or problem you face... from a lack of motivation to regular schedule disruptions, help give you the strength and drive to push through and overcome those challenges.

So, now...this minute...think about the goals you've set for yourself and why you've set that goal. And, if you haven't before, connect that goal to your values, the things that you care about at your core, the things that make you, you. That connection won't guarantee success, but it will undoubtedly maximize the likelihood that you'll ultimately achieve the goals you've set out to achieve.

11

Stop Whining

"When you complain, you make yourself a victim. Leave the situation, change the situation, or accept it. All else is madness." – Eckhart Tolle

We complain WAY too often. In some ways, this is not our fault. Our brain is biased to notice and place a lot more importance on things that are wrong with our environments and with ourselves than on things are right. This is known as the negativity bias.

Noticing things that are wrong is not, in and of itself, a bad thing because noticing them allows us to fix them. However, when we habitually and regularly tune in to those things that aren't the way we'd like them to be, we doom ourselves to far more anxiety, stress, and fear than is necessary or useful.

When you catch yourself whining about these bad things in your life, realize the futility of this behavior. Realize that the whining and complaining accomplish nothing but bringing down your mood and the moods of those you're complaining to. Then, stop complaining and change the way you're choosing to view your situation.

Choose to notice those things that are going well. Recognize and celebrate the strengths that you have. Appreciate the friends and family around you who care about you and support you regularly.

Complaining accomplishes nothing. Instead, change how you perceive the situation, generate potential solutions and ways forward, and then get to work.

12

Motivation – Levels

"Understanding motivation is one of the most important things we can do in our lives, because it has such a bearing on why we do the things we do and whether we enjoy them or not."
– Clayton Christensen

Motivation is essential for achieving not just big, long-term goals that we set but for sustaining day-to-day behaviors required to keep our lives functioning normally. Whether trying to get a college degree or simply get dinner on the table and the laundry done, motivation is necessary to accomplish what we set out to accomplish.

As you move through your day, if you find your motivation levels low…your drive to do what you know you should do waning… and you're not sure exactly why, I encourage you to ask and answer three questions. The answers to these questions will open your eyes to why you lack motivation.

• Do I believe I can successfully do what I know I should do? How confident am I that I can do what needs to be done capably and competently? If you're not confident about your abilities, that may explain your low motivation. Few people are motivated to do things they aren't confident they can do successfully.

- Do I care? Does the behavior or activity matter to me for some reason? If not, your motivation is likely to be low because who gets motivated to do something they care nothing about or think is unimportant? Nobody.

- Does the benefit outweigh the cost? If not, that may explain your lack of motivation. You might care about and believe you're fully capable of accomplishing the task, but if the cost of doing that activity (e.g., time, money, effort) outweighs the benefits, your motivation will likely be low.

Things we know need to be done fill our personal and professional lives; however, when motivation is low, getting done what needs to be done becomes a tremendous struggle. Hopefully, answering the three questions above can help you pinpoint exactly why your motivation levels are low and give you some ideas about how to address whatever factors are keeping you from achieving what you set out to achieve.

13

Values

"The strengths of a man's virtue should not be measured by his special exertions, but by his habitual acts." – Blaise Pascal

Each of us has a set of values by which we try to live our lives. Values are those things we strive for or aspire to, the ways that we believe we should be, others should be, and the world at large should be.

Some of us keep our core values in the forefront of our minds, while others of us have our values operating primarily from our subconscious. Some of us may be living by values we've "picked up" throughout our lives (e.g., from our parents, books, culture), while others of us have adopted a specifically defined set of values aligned with organizations (e.g., Army Values - loyalty, duty, respect, selfless service, honor, integrity, personal courage), philosophies (e.g., Stoic Values/Virtues - wisdom, courage, justice, moderation/temperance), religions (e.g., Christianity, Judaism, Hinduism, Taoism, Islam), or purely secular sources (e.g., Benjamin Franklin's Thirteen Virtues – temperance, silence, order, resolution, justice, sincerity, moderation, chastity, humility, tranquility, frugality, industry, and sincerity).

Regardless of how we came to adopt our values, those values influence every facet of our lives. Our values affect the friends we have, the activities we enjoy, the books and movies we choose, and every decision we make. Our values color our thoughts and perceptions of every situation, so the emotions we experience and our reactions to things that happen daily are, intentionally or unintentionally, affected by our values.

Right now, as you're reading this piece, think about your values. If identifying your core values is challenging, it might help to look at some of the examples above. Once you've clearly identified at least one or two of those values you hold most dear...those values that define you, are part of you, and make you who you are at your core...write them down somewhere and keep them easily accessible and in the forefront of your mind. See if you can recognize those values at work in your perceptions and judgments of yourself, others, and the world at large.

14

Managing Emotions

"Destructive thoughts and emotions undermine the very causes of peace and happiness. If you think clearly about it, it makes no sense to think you're seeking happiness, if you do nothing to restrain angry, spiteful, and malicious thoughts and emotions." – Dalai Lama

As human beings, we experience emotions constantly, and sometimes these emotions…particularly the negative ones (ones we don't like to experience)…become so powerful that they cause a great deal of stress and significantly hinder our lives. When this happens, try one…or all three…of the following methods for managing these emotions.

Mindfulness – Take a moment to simply sit with the emotion. Don't fight it, judge it, or try to get rid of it. Simply recognize the emotion, name it, and inspect it with a sense of curiosity and interest. Engaging with emotions in this way can reduce the strength and power of the emotion and allow us to gain some insight into why we are experiencing that emotion. Emotions are finite, transient, impermanent things. By simply sitting with the emotion in this non-judgmental way, the emotion will gradually diminish in strength and eventually disappear altogether over time.

Examine the Thought/Emotion Connection – According to cognitive psychologists, emotions emerge from our interpretations of our experiences. That is, the meaning we assign to events in our lives, the way we perceive and understand things that happen to us, determines the type and strength of our emotions. So, take a moment to ask yourself why you feel the way you do. For example, if you feel afraid, do you perceive some sort of threat? If you feel angry, do you believe that someone or something (e.g., an organization) harmed you or did something wrong to you? By recognizing our emotions and then examining the perceptions and meanings of events that are driving those emotions, we can gain a much clearer understanding of why we feel the emotion we do and, therefore, what actions we can take to deal productively with our situation.

Breathing – When experiencing powerful emotions, simply engaging in deep breathing and focusing our attention directly on the breath can help us weather the storm of powerful emotions. When breathing deeply, from the diaphragm, and rhythmically, we stimulate our vagus nerve and activate our parasympathetic nervous system...the part of our autonomic nervous system responsible for calm recovery. Also, because we can only truly focus on one thing at a time, focusing our attention fully and completely on the breath has the added bonus of taking our attention off of both the cause of the emotion and the emotion itself.

Any one of these methods for regulating emotion can be helpful by itself, but it's possible to use more than one, or even all three, of these methods simultaneously. For example, you can begin by intentionally breathing deeply and focusing solely on your breath (Breathing). Then, while continuing your deep, rhythmic breathing, you can turn your attention to the emotion, naming it, and examining it in a curious and non-judgmental way (Mindfulness). Finally, continuing to breathe, you can ask yourself how you are currently thinking about and understanding your current circumstances to gain insight into why the emotion emerged in the first place.

By using one or more of these strategies, you can effectively manage your emotions, more thoroughly understand your emotions, and transition into a mental and emotional state that allows you to engage with life effectively and productively.

15

Motivation – What is Your WHY?

"If you are working on something that you really care about, you don't have to be pushed. the vision pulls you." – Steve Jobs

How motivated we are is determined by three things: 1) Our belief in our ability to succeed, 2) Our belief that the benefit of engaging in the activity outweighs the cost, and 3) The extent to which we care about the activity (Our WHY). However, even if our motivation levels are high, our WHY is still incredibly important.

Tasks/Activities/Goals can matter to us for a number of reasons. For example, you might care about a task because of a reward you'll get if you complete the task successfully; to avoid looking bad compared to…or in the eyes of…other people; or because the task has personal meaning and importance to you.

It turns out that when we care about an activity because we strongly believe in its meaning and importance, it aligns with a central value or purpose we hold, and it's something we're doing because of who we believe ourselves to be at our core…we try harder, persist longer, overcome challenges more consistently, perform better, and enjoy ourselves more than when our WHY stems merely from attempts to obtain rewards or avoid looking bad.

Today, regardless of how big or small your tasks/activities/goals are, take time to ask yourself why these goals matter to you. And if the answer to that question involves things outside of yourself (e.g., rewards, others' opinions), see if you can assign a deeper, more personal meaning to the task/activity/goal. See if you can assign it a WHY in line with your core values, the things that drive your everyday attitudes and behaviors…the things that make you, you. Then notice how much more easily you can maintain the motivation to start those tasks/activities/goals…and how often you finish them.

16

Fight Inertia

"Nothing happens until something moves." – Albert Einstein

I nertia is the tendency for a body in motion to stay in motion and a body at rest to stay at rest unless acted on by an outside force. Inertia is most often discussed in terms of physics but is relevant in our everyday lives as well.

For example, think about behaviors you would like to change, maybe even have made some effort to change, and how challenging that change is. It might be eating habits, social media scrolling, or stopping for that $4 cup of coffee every morning. Whatever the behavior, it's one that you're comfortable with. Your body is in motion, and it will stay that way unless active, deliberate force is applied to redirect that behavior.

Similarly, think about a behavior you'd like to start (e.g., exercising more) or a goal you'd like to begin pursuing (e.g., getting a degree). In this case, your body is at rest and will stay that way "unless acted on by an outside force".

The "outside force" applied to either redirect unwanted behavior or initiate desired behavior can take many different forms. It might be support from a friend, constant reminders to yourself about why you want the behavior to change, acquiring more information, or immediate and acute negative consequences associated with the behavior (e.g., bad news from a doctor). The bottom line, though, is that combatting counterproductive inertia requires something different to occur, something that is not currently happening, for you to move in a more productive direction.

Where is inertia the guiding force within your life? Where are you stuck in place or headed in a direction you know is not the best direction for you or your family? What "outside force" can you lean on to help you fight the inertia that's holding you back?

17

Present Moment – Hope and Fear

"[Hope and Fear] belong to a mind in suspense, to a mind in a state of anxiety through looking into the future. Both are mainly due to projecting our thoughts far ahead of us instead of adapting ourselves to the present." – Lucius Annaeus Seneca

Although thinking ahead to plan and prepare for upcoming events is unquestionably beneficial, we often find ourselves fixated on the future in ways that, ultimately, can create suffering for ourselves. For example, thinking about possible outcomes of actions we might take may lead to worry, anxiety, and fear. And, while immersing ourselves in the hope that the future will be different from…better than…the present, we are, by definition, considering our current circumstances bad enough to warrant the change we hope for. In both cases, we experience the anxiety and unhappiness Seneca discussed in the quote above.

Today, engage in the necessary planning for future events by examining the facts of your situation as objectively as possible. However, once plans have been created and decisions have been made, turn your attention immediately back to the present moment. Avoid lingering in the future, and be especially wary of repeatedly creating and playing out "what if" scenarios. Whether the scenarios generate hope or fear, they take your attention away from both the concrete steps you can take in the present moment to affect the future and your appreciation of what, in this present moment, is worthy of appreciation. In other words, by fixating on the future, we become blind to opportunities for change and the goodness and well-being accessible in the here and now.

There is no need to transform possible suffering in the future into actual suffering in the present.

18

Hedonic Treadmill

"Folks are usually about as happy as they make their minds up to be."
– Abraham Lincoln

From time immemorial, human beings have been pursuing happiness and well-being. Although definitions abound, the one that has stood the test of time is the concept of eudaimonia, usually understood in terms of flourishing or thriving. Eudaimonia can be compared to hedonism, understood typically as the maximization of pleasure and the minimization of pain or discomfort.

Often, we set our sights on a goal (e.g., college degree), object (e.g., house), or state of being (e.g., married) and tell ourselves that once we achieve this end state, we will be happy. Once I get that degree, then I'll be satisfied. As soon as I can buy a house, I'll be happy. If only I can find the "right one" and get married, then life would be content. And you know what? You're right…if you define happiness in terms of hedonism.

When we base our happiness on outcomes, "things" we pursue, we can absolutely expect a temporary boost in happiness once we get that "thing." However, we can just as certainly expect that happiness to diminish over a relatively short period of time, our happiness levels to return to what they were before getting that "thing," and a return of the desire to pursue some other "thing" in an effort to regain the happiness we experienced before. This cycle of dissatisfaction/wanting, pursuing, getting, happiness/pleasure, dissatisfaction/wanting…is known as the *Hedonic Treadmill.*

To experience eudaimonia, we need to base our happiness and well-being on more predictable, consistent factors than the attainment of goals or obtainment of objects. Instead, happiness must stem from our everyday experiences, from what's happening in the present moment. Happiness must come from what we pay attention to and appreciate the here and now. The present moment is where thriving and flourishing occur.

Today, periodically, take time to evaluate your mood. If you recognize that you're not as happy as you'd like to be, pause and notice something in your immediate environment that you appreciate. Or, bring to mind something or someone in your life you're truly grateful for. Focus on this thing or individual for just a few minutes, and then re-evaluate your mood. Are you happier? These everyday things that can bring us immediate joy are always accessible. Therefore, happiness is always accessible. We just need to decide to access it.

19

Time

"I believe that every human being has a finite number of heartbeats. I don't intend to waste any of mine running around doing exercises." – Neil Armstrong

Time is the most precious commodity we have. Of all the resources we regularly seek out and use, time is the only one that is impossible to supplement.

It's not that we don't pay attention to time. On the contrary, we often pay a great deal of attention to time. We rush around trying to be places on time, and we even worry about wasting time. The problem is that our evaluations of whether or not we're "wasting time" typically are done in terms of *quantity* of time spent, the amount of time we take to achieve what we want to achieve, rather than *quality* of time, the things we're choosing to spend time on in the first place.

Today, periodically pause and reflect on how you are using your time. Then, consider your priorities and values, the things that are truly important to you, and ask yourself if your use of time right now is in line with those priorities. Is what you're doing something that really matters to you? If not, do something that does.

Our time on this planet is limited, and we don't know how much of it we have. So, instead of emphasizing getting as much done as possible with the finite time we have, let's focus on spending our time in ways and with people that are most important to us.

20

Behavior – Check Under the Water

"Human behavior flows from three main sources: desire, emotions, and knowledge." – Plato

"People say I make strange choices, but they're not strange for me. My sickness is that I'm fascinated by human behavior, by what's underneath the surface, by the worlds inside people." – Johnny Depp

The behavior of others constantly impacts us. Whether talking about the behavior of strangers, friends, coworkers, or family members, these behaviors can affect us in a variety of ways. They might be helpful, annoying, surprising, frustrating, or relieving…the effects they have on us can run the gamut. However, in these moments, it's important to remember that the behavior itself is only the outward result of deeper processes operating inside that individual.

For example, if you witness a person yelling at a server in a restaurant, that behavior isn't just happening in isolation and out of the blue. It's happening because of the emotions that individual is experiencing, which, in turn, are the result of how that individual interprets, perceives, and understands that situation. Further, those interpretations and perceptions are influenced by that individual's mood at the time of the incident and that individual's values and beliefs about the nature of the world and others. Even further, those values and beliefs came into being primarily because of the lessons taught to that person by other people and the environment in which that individual was raised. The point here is that MANY factors influence the behaviors we witness every day.

This information doesn't excuse inappropriate, inconsiderate, or dangerous behavior. However, understanding that behaviors are, in many ways, simply the tip of the iceberg allows us to be more thoughtful and deliberative in our assessment of the situation and more compassionate toward others.

Since we know that there's more going on under the surface driving behavior, we can question our initial impressions to ensure we have as complete and accurate a picture of what's going on as possible. Also, because we realize that people (ourselves included) regularly deal with many challenges and emotions, we can be more compassionate when those moods, challenges, and emotions impact people in counterproductive ways.

So, as you move through your day and witness the cornucopia of behaviors people all around you engage in, keep in mind the part of the iceberg you can't see, that part underneath that's actually responsible for the behavior you're witnessing. Recognize that what you're seeing is more complicated than an initial glance and impression can elucidate. Remember times when you yourself have behaved in regretful ways because of strong emotions. And exhibit compassion by giving that person the benefit of the doubt. Again, people should be held accountable for their inappropriate behavior, but judging and condemning other people as a result of momentary choices, particularly given that each of us has been carried away by emotions in very similar ways, can lead to mistaken, unfair conclusions.

21

Acceptance – Focus on the Present

"For after all, the best thing one can do when it's raining is let it rain."
- Henry Wadsworth Longfellow

Unwanted things happen all the time that we have absolutely no control over. These things make us angry, sad, or frustrated and wreak havoc with our meticulously made plans…and there's nothing we can do about it. In those situations, there are really only two things we can do: 1) Wish things were different, or 2) Accept how things are.

We might dwell on all the things we think could have happened differently to change the situation or things we could have done that we believe would have altered our circumstances. We could spend a lot of time living in the past and making up stories that will never manifest in reality. However, this path leads to misery, regret, guilt, shame, and a complete lack of productivity.

On the other hand, we could pause to examine and thoroughly

understand our present circumstances and accept things as they currently are. That is, we can exist in the present with an accurate picture of our current challenges, focus directly on those aspects of the situation we can influence, and take purposeful action. This path leads to persistence, grit, and productivity.

Today, when things don't go exactly the way you wanted them to go, pay attention to your reaction. Are you wallowing in self-pity and creating alternate scenarios that would require a time machine to do you any good? Or, are you acknowledging the reality of your circumstances, honestly assessing the situation, and turning your attention toward affecting positive change in ways that are possible for you in that moment?

To use Longfellow's example above…are you wishing for the sun while getting drenched? Or, are you looking for shelter that will keep you dry and warm?

22

Mindset

"When you enter a mindset, you enter a new world. In one world (the world of fixed traits) success is about proving you're smart or talented. Validating yourself. In the other (the world of changing qualities) it's about stretching yourself to learn something new. Developing yourself." - Carol Dweck

In 2007, Dr. Carol Dweck introduced the concepts of fixed and growth mindsets and described how these two very different mindsets influence us in various areas of our lives.

A fixed mindset describes the belief that change, growth, and development ARE NOT possible. A person with a fixed mindset believes that their brains and bodies are wired how they're wired. As a result, the best one can do is to be aware of one's strengths and weaknesses and make choices and engage in behaviors that maximize the former and minimize the latter.

A growth mindset describes the belief that change, growth, and development ARE possible. A person with a growth mindset believes that although they are strong and weak in some areas right now, they can improve. As a result, the best one can do is to identify what one would like to improve; set goals for what one would like to achieve; and invest the time, attention, and effort necessary to move oneself closer to that desired state.

People with a fixed mindset tend to avoid risk because failure is seen as indicative of a personal defect wired directly into them, whereas growth mindset people accept risk because failure is seen as feedback they can use to grow and improve regardless of whether they achieved what they set out to achieve. People with a fixed mindset tend to avoid effort and evaluate their performances in terms of *how little* effort it took to achieve a standard, whereas people with a growth mindset value effort and evaluate their performances in terms of *how much* effort they exerted. People with a fixed mindset tend to view improvement-related feedback as a personal attack and evidence that they are not good enough, whereas people with a growth mindset tend to welcome improvement-related feedback and use that feedback as just one more resource they can leverage toward personal growth.

Today, as you flow through different areas of your life (e.g., parent, employee), notice which mindset you've adopted. Notice whether you believe that more knowledge and effort will lead to improvement or will make no difference in your current proficiency levels. Notice whether you welcome feedback and think carefully about how to apply that feedback in ways that can help you improve or become defensive and anxious when receiving feedback that does not focus solely on how well you did.

Human beings are in a constant state of change. Stagnation is impossible. We are either moving forward or backward; we never stay in the same place. We are made for growth and adaptation, and a growth mindset goes a long way toward using our natural tendencies to help us develop and improve in efficient and effective ways.

23

Perfectionism

"Perfectionism is an internalized oppression." – Gloria Steinham

Many people describe themselves as perfectionists without really understanding what that term implies or how detrimental it can be.

World-renowned emotions researcher Brene Brown defines *perfectionism* as "a self-destructive and addictive belief system that fuels this primary thought: If I look perfect, live perfectly, work perfectly, and do everything perfectly, I can avoid or minimize the painful feelings of shame, judgment, and blame."

Perfectionism is a mindset that is focused primarily on what other people think. Perfectionists believe that success…and, therefore, acceptance and respect…depends on unfailingly meeting expectations they set for themselves…and believe others have set for them. Because their self-identities and self-worth are tied to meeting those expectations, the bar that perfectionists set for themselves tends to be easily reachable…at least for them. This is to help ensure success and avoid failure and can result in what

Brown refers to as *life paralysis.*

Life paralysis refers to all the opportunities we miss out on and dreams we fail to pursue because of a fear of imperfection, mistakes, and…thus…disappointing other people and looking bad in other people's eyes. Perfectionists are very hesitant to come outside of their comfort zones and take risks because those risks might entail looking bad and, as a result, being judged by others to be incompetent or defective in some way. Therefore, since stepping outside our comfort zones is what makes improvement possible, perfectionists have a tough time developing or improving in any facet of their lives.

If you know you have perfectionist tendencies, challenge yourself today to do three things. First, pay careful attention to the number of people around you regularly making mistakes. Notice the people who spill or drop something, trip over a curb, mix up their words, or burn dinner. Then, notice how those people react to their mistake and, more importantly, how others react to the mistake that was made. What you will begin to see is that mistakes are simply one behavior at one point in time that are usually able to be rectified and rarely, if ever, indicative of an inherent personality flaw.

Second, try to do something you would like to do but haven't tried because you were afraid you might fail. When you inevitably make a mistake, avoid viewing that mistake as an indicator of your intrinsic inadequacy. Instead, choose to view that mistake as a learning opportunity…then try again.

Finally, each time you catch yourself falling into a perfectionist mindset, remind yourself that your worth does not depend on others' opinions. Remind yourself, too, about the concept of life paralysis and how boring life would be if you limited yourself only to things you can already do exceptionally well!

24

Choose Good Habits

"Your net worth to the world is usually determined by what remains after your bad habits are subtracted from your good ones." -Benjamin Franklin

Neuroplasticity refers to the brain's ability to rewire itself to make whatever neural connections it makes most often more efficient. Thoughts, feelings, and behaviors are simply patterns of neural connections. So, when we engage in any behavior multiple times, for example, the same neurons are firing in the same pattern, and as the saying goes, "Neurons that fire together, wire together." Over time and enough repetitions, these neural firing patterns become second nature and happen very quickly and efficiently. When this happens, we tend to refer to it as "muscle memory" or habit.

Humans are creatures of habit because our brains attempt to create as predictable and efficient a world for us as possible. Habits are ubiquitous and can be "good" or "bad"…that is, useful/ not useful, productive/counterproductive. Depending on what articles you read, habits tend to take between 30-60 days to take hold solidly. Since neuroplasticity is simply a natural feature of our brains and habits are the inevitable result, it behooves us to take advantage of these facts by deliberately creating helpful and beneficial habits by intentionally and repeatedly engaging in the types of thoughts and behaviors we want.

Today, tune into your habits. Pay attention to things as simple as how you dry off after a shower (try doing it differently…it's interesting) or how you brush your teeth. Pay attention, too, to the types of thoughts or perceptions you have that might be habitual. For example, notice the thoughts you have when the notion of going to work or certain people in your world comes to mind. Notice how easily and frequently the same types of thoughts come to you and how predictable the emotions that follow those thoughts are.

Also, think about ways you might like to change…things you might want to learn or improve; stuff you might like to reprioritize; or ways of perceiving, understanding, or interacting with the world you would like to be different. Then, make a deliberate effort to make your thoughts and behaviors match what you want them to be. It will be hard and might feel unnatural or disingenuous at the beginning, but stick with it for 30-60 days and notice how much more quickly and regularly those thoughts, perceptions, and behaviors tend to manifest themselves.

25

Fighting the Confirmation Bias

"It's not what you look at that matters, it's what you see." – Henry
-David Thoreau

We all have core values and beliefs that heavily influence how we perceive our environments. One of the ways this influence occurs is through something called the confirmation bias.

The confirmation bias is our tendency to confirm what we already believe. When we hold strong beliefs about ourselves, others, or the world at large, we notice, remember, and place a lot of importance on evidence that supports those beliefs. At the same time, however, we also place very little importance on, don't remember, or overlook altogether evidence that does NOT support our beliefs. As a result, we see exactly what we expect to see.

Because of the confirmation bias, we can be so certain of the truth of our perceptions that it closes us off to the possibility that we might either be wrong or, at the very least, not getting a complete picture of our situation. Therefore, it is essential that we regularly question our assumptions and perceptions and recognize the possibility that, because of how the confirmation bias is operating on our beliefs, we might be missing critical information, information that might very well alter the ways we choose to respond to other people or circumstances.

Today, notice those times when you are certain that you are right, when you're sure you have a completely accurate picture of reality. Once you recognize those times, ask yourself a few questions: 1) Am I seeing what I expect to see? 2) Does what I'm seeing confirm what I already believe to be true? 3) Is there any information that I'm missing? 4) How do others see or perceive this situation? The same way I do? 5) Is it possible to perceive the situation differently?

Asking and answering these questions will help you fight the confirmation bias by opening your mind up to the possibility that more information might exist and, therefore, a more thorough and accurate understanding of the situation is possible. And with this more comprehensive and correct comprehension of your circumstances, you will be able to act and interact in ways that are productive and helpful for yourself and for those you care about.

26

Rejuvenation

"Each person deserves a day away in which no problems are confronted, no solutions searched for. Each of us needs to withdraw from the cares which will not withdraw from us." – Maya Angelou

Although our society glorifies continual effort, work, and progress toward something…anything, it's necessary to balance those pursuits with times of recovery, refreshment, and rejuvenation.

Pursuing goals and focusing on efficiency and effectiveness in our efforts is not necessarily bad. Having clearly defined goals and daily activities we can focus on that help us achieve those goals ensures that our finite time on this Earth is spent in ways that are important, valuable, and personally meaningful to ourselves and those around us. When this pursuit of efficiency and expeditiousness becomes a problem, however, is when we fail to build in time for reflection and rejuvenation.

From both physical and mental standpoints, we require time to recover. We need time for our bodies to rebuild muscle tissue that has been literally ripped to shreds during physical activity and our minds to process and coalesce all of the information we've learned during our personal and professional pursuits.

This recovery and rejuvenation time is a natural and essential part of our human cycle; however, it can sometimes be challenging to recognize when we've reached the point when we need to prioritize active recovery over energetic goal pursuit.

Today, periodically tune into your mind and body and pay attention to what each is telling you about its condition. If you're tired, your body is sore, and you notice a general feeling of physical weakness or fatigue, you probably need physical rest. If you find it hard to concentrate, remember things you believe you should be able to recall easily, or generate and follow logical thought patterns, you probably need some mental rest.

Regular recovery is critical for our overall well-being. If you want to maximize the efficiency and effectiveness of your various pursuits, prioritize time for rejuvenation.

27

What is Success?

"Success is falling nine times and getting up ten." - Jon Bon Jovi

"Failure is success if we learn from it." - Malcolm Forbes

"Success isn't about how much money you make. It's about the difference you make in people's lives." - Michelle Obama

There are many ways to define success. Some people define success in terms of the achievement (or not) of long-term, challenging goals, while others measure success in terms of how many things they check off their "to-do" list each day. Some people define success in terms of how they compare to others, while other people measure success in terms of whether they surpass their own previous efforts. Some people determine success by the number of bad things they avoid rather than good things they achieve, while other people don't define success in terms of achievement at all but, instead, in terms of mindsets and attitudes (e.g., compassion, empathy, confidence) they adopt and sustain throughout the day.

How do you typically define success?

Take a minute to think about how you know whether you have been successful. Are there other ways to assess the extent to which you've been successful? Are there aspects of your life that might benefit from a different definition of success?

28

Achieve Goals with Attitudes and Mindsets

"The greatest discovery of my generation is that human beings can alter their lives by altering their attitudes of mind." -William James

L ong-term goals are achieved by consistently completing small, daily activities; however, the daily activities are only completed when proper attitudes and mindsets are adopted.

Whatever your long-term goal is, you will not achieve it because of the periodic accomplishment of large, significant actions, and you certainly won't achieve it in one fell swoop. The achievement of any long-term goal results from regular, reliable, and consistent small actions that bring one continually closer to the desired end-state. To persistently pursue these small but vital daily activities, however, we must maintain a mindset focused on growth and development and an attitude grounded in confidence and perseverance.

The attitudes we adopt and the mindsets we choose exert

significant power over the things we focus on, how we perceive those things, and the behaviors we select. The great thing, though, is that our attitudes and mindsets are in our control. We decide how we view and react to failure, uncertainty, and low motivation. We determine if we will choose courage over comfort, effort over procrastination, and grit and perseverance over buckling and giving in.

What attitudes and mindsets do you most often adopt when considering your daily goal pursuit? Are there certain situations that make fostering and maintaining productive attitudes and mindsets more difficult than others? Do you find that it's easier to sustain helpful attitudes and mindsets with some goals, or around certain people, than others?

Goal achievement is, in large part, the result of tenacity. Little by little, we narrow the gap between where we are and where we want to be. We narrow that gap by engaging in the daily behaviors necessary for growth and development; however, those daily behaviors are only possible to the extent that our attitudes and mindsets allow us to engage in those behaviors regularly, dependably, and effectively.

29

Follow Life's Prescriptions

"When one door of happiness closes, another opens; but often we look so long at the closed door that we do not see the one which has been opened for us." Helen Keller

Every day, without fail, we encounter unforeseen circumstances, things we hadn't planned on or considered while imagining how our day would go. When these surprise events occur, we often fight against our new, unexpected reality. We complain about the unfairness of the situation, wish fervently that it hadn't happened, and imagine how much better life would be if things had turned out differently. Rather than adopt this unhelpful perspective, try thinking about the unexpected event as something Life has prescribed for you.

When you have something wrong with you and go to the doctor, the doctor prescribes something they think will fix whatever the problem is. This prescription might be taking a drug, wearing an apparatus, or some other sort of behavior. Sometimes, however, doctors prescribe things that don't make intuitive sense. For example, you might go to the doctor because of shoulder pain, and the doctor prescribes physical therapy that, when done correctly and to standard, makes your shoulder hurt worse than it did before going to the doctor. This kind of prescription is counterintuitive, but we trust the doctor, believe in their diagnosis and judgment, and engage in the prescribed behavior whether it makes sense to us at that moment or not. We can think about life's events in the same way.

Today, when those unexpected challenges arise, try thinking about them as prescriptions from Life. Think about them as situations that will help you develop and improve and that you will ultimately benefit from in the long run. If you're stuck in unanticipated traffic, think of it as a prescription for patience. If your child brings home subpar work from school, think of it as a prescription for communication. If your spouse changes dinner plans due to uncontrollable factors at work, think of it as a prescription for compassion.

Life will predictably and inevitably throw unexpected situations at us. The more we can view those situations not as obstacles and hindrances to our progress and well-being but as opportunities for growth and improvement, the happier and less stressed out we will be.

30

The Nature of Thoughts

"Perception is reality, but it may not be actuality..." - Bill Cowher

The nature of thoughts is complex. On the one hand, thoughts are ephemeral, fleeting, temporary things that suddenly manifest themselves in our awareness and just as suddenly disappear, usually replaced by yet another equally evanescent thought. On the other hand, thoughts are what create our realities. Our perceptions, understandings, and explanations of the world around us, other people, and ourselves are all thoughts. Our entire existence is defined by nothing more, or less, than thoughts.

Thankfully, thoughts are temporary. That means that if we recognize thoughts that are not helpful, we can let those thoughts go and direct our minds toward more helpful thoughts, more productive ways of thinking about our current situations. This works because thoughts are simply thoughts; they are not representative of the true nature of our existence. Our current circumstances, things that happen to us, interactions we have with others...all of these can be thought about and perceived in a cornucopia of ways. No one thought at any given moment accurately and fully represents reality as it truly is. It's simply one of many interpretations of reality possible at that specific moment in time.

Throughout your day, take a moment now and then to examine your thinking. Recognize the variety of thoughts you have from one moment to the next. Notice how quickly and seemingly out of nowhere thoughts appear. Notice also how quickly, of their own accord, and with no effort from you thoughts disappear. Try acknowledging a thought when it arises as simply a temporary thought and gently redirecting your mind toward a different thought, a different way of seeing a situation, a different point of focus and attention. Notice how your mind creates thoughts of its own accord and how we can deliberately choose certain thoughts that serve our purposes in those moments.

As human beings, we can't prevent thoughts from happening. However, we can avoid identifying ourselves with those thoughts and giving them more power than they deserve. We can recognize thoughts for what they truly are, temporary perceptions that appear and disappear regularly and rapidly. We can acknowledge and gently allow thoughts that don't serve us to disappear while deliberately cultivating thoughts that benefit ourselves and those around us.

31

Perception is Reality

"All our knowledge has its origins in our perceptions." - Leonardo Da Vinci

The reality we experience results solely from how we interpret, explain, and understand the world around us. This means that we create and can control our own realities. This knowledge also explains why other people may not view things the same way we do and lead to more empathy and compassion.

What we experience as reality is simply our perception of the stimuli in our environments that make it into our attentional awareness. We are bombarded constantly with all forms of stimuli (e.g., auditory, kinesthetic, visual, olfactory), and our brains are incapable of processing all of these stimuli. So, only a very limited amount of the stimuli make it into our conscious awareness. The stimuli that DO make it into our awareness are interpreted and explained by us in ways unique to us. These interpretations are influenced by our beliefs, values, and past experiences and form the basis for our overall reality.

As human beings, though, we can focus our attention deliberately and intentionally choose how we think about those things we experience. Therefore, we can direct and control our own sense of what is "real" and "true".

Today, stop and notice where your attention is focused at any given time and how you are experiencing...how you are perceiving...that situation. Then, deliberately choose to attend to another aspect of the situation, prioritize a different feature within your environment, and notice how your understanding of the situation changes. Finally, keep your attention on any aspect of a situation you want (e.g., how someone is driving in front of you; the tone of voice someone is using) and choose to explain that facet of your experience differently. Instead of explaining erratic driving as someone being an inconsiderate jerk, explain it in terms of the person trying to make it home as fast as possible with medicine for a sick child. Instead of understanding a tone of voice as angry and demeaning, try to view the tone of voice as the result of fear and uncertainty.

By recognizing that we create our own realities through our perceptions, we open ourselves up to endless opportunities to enhance our own well-being. And the knowledge that others are perceiving situations in their own unique ways enables us to be more sensitive to the possibility that factors we're unaware of influence others' actions and attitudes. As a result, empathy and compassion are much easier to extend.

32

Changing Your Past

"When I was younger, I could remember anything…whether it had happened or not." - Mark Twain

Many people say that we should focus solely on the present moment, because the present moment is the only moment we can control. We can't change what has already occurred, and the future will result from actions taken in the present. I understand this perspective, but I disagree…I think you CAN change the past.

What we think of as "the past" is largely just a series of memories, and memories are complicated things. First, our memories are notoriously inaccurate. Second, memories become less accurate each time we pull them up in our minds. Third, memories can only consist of things that we paid enough attention to for them to end up being stored in our minds long-term. Finally, memories don't consist of carefully cataloged data and facts. Memories are, instead, colored and influenced heavily by our emotional state at the time of the event and how we perceived the event when it initially occurred. That is, we remember experiences rather than facts, and our experiences are determined by where our attention was focused and how we understood the event. This is why two people who experienced the exact same thing at the exact same time can have very different memories of, and feelings about, that event. Each person's attention may have been focused on different aspects of the environment, and/or each person's interpretation of...the meaning they assigned to...what they paid attention to might be very different.

How does this relate to my claim that we can change the past?

Because our memories of the past are largely the result of our perceptions of past events, we can change the past by changing our perceptions. We can change the past by prioritizing different aspects of a past situation and interpreting those aspects differently from how we've interpreted them before.

We can also choose to assign different meaning and importance to past events. For example, if I got a divorce five years ago, I might remember that event as very painful in many ways and, therefore, remember the divorce as a terrible thing I wish hadn't happened. However, I can change my focus from the pain associated with the divorce to the freedom and opportunity to connect with other people and engage in other activities in ways that would not have been possible if still married. In this way, I can "change the past", because I can alter how I remember the divorce. My memory of the divorce will be different because I will have changed what was important to me about it. Therefore, my new perception and perspective will result in different memories when I remember the divorce.

Although it's true we can't change the actual events that occurred in our lives...five years ago or five minutes ago, it's also true that we can perceive those events any way we want. Which facets of those events we focus on and the meaning that we assign to the events themselves are completely within our control and can be changed whenever we choose.

Today, experiment with "changing your past". Bring to mind a memory that causes you suffering and try to reimagine that event in ways that elicit different thoughts and feelings. See if you can intentionally change the things within the memory that you focus on and prioritize. Deliberately make an effort to alter the meaning of what happened in a way that results, for all intents and purposes, in a new memory. Remember your past in a way that is helpful and beneficial for you.

33

Stop Blaming Your Emotions On Other People and Things

"There is nothing either good or bad but thinking makes it so."
-Shakespeare

When something happens in our lives, we experience emotions and engage in behaviors directly related to that event. For example, when we get stuck at a light, our kids are rude to us, or we are tasked with a time-sensitive assignment at work, we might feel irritated, disappointed, and nervous. Indeed, even imagining these scenarios may be enough for you to experience similar emotions. However, this connection between the event and the emotions we experience is not quite so simple. Understanding that connection requires us to recognize a critical component we often fail to consider...our perception of the event.

Events in and of themselves are neither good nor bad; they just are. They are composed of simple, straightforward facts. The way we perceive or interpret these facts, though...the meaning that we assign to the events that occur... that's what determines the feelings we experience.

For example, I might feel irritated or frustrated if I'm stuck at a light. I might also feel grateful, because that extra time sitting still allows me to find something new to listen to, organize something in the front seat, or simply breathe and relax. In this scenario, whether I experience irritation or gratitude is entirely the result of how I choose to perceive my situation. Similarly, if my child is rude to me, I might feel anger or annoyance. I might also feel disappointment or guilt (e.g., "how did I manage to raise a child who acts like this?"). Again, the emotions I experience depend entirely on my interpretation of the event, how I see and understand and explain what's going on.

Today, recognize those situations in which you are explaining your emotions in terms of the event that just occurred. Then, pursue the source of that emotion further by asking, "What is it about this event that is driving this emotion?" "What does this situation mean to me, and how is that meaning affecting my feelings in this moment?" "Is there another way of perceiving this situation? A way of understanding what's going in that will drive a different emotion?"

Asking these questions will help you uncover the real force behind your emotions…your perceptions and interpretations of the circumstances you experience. Then, because we can control our perceptions and how we view our circumstances, we can choose perceptions that drive helpful, productive emotions rather than painful, counterproductive ones.

34

Cultivate Gratitude

"Let us rise up and be thankful, for if we didn't learn a lot today, at least we learned a little, and if we didn't learn a little, at least we didn't get sick, and if we got sick, at least we didn't die; so, let us all be thankful." – Buddha

One of the best ways to immediately get rid of negative emotions is to elicit feelings of gratitude.

Regardless of what negative emotion you're experiencing (e.g., anger, anxiety, disappointment), bringing to mind something you are grateful for can quickly alleviate those negative emotions and give you an entirely different perspective on your situation.

Emotions are the result of our perceptions of whatever we happen to be focused on. If we believe we've lost something that matters a lot to us, we are likely to feel sad. If we believe we've been harmed or treated wrongly, we will likely feel angry. The fact is, though, that we can perceive our environment in any way we choose. Therefore, instead of interpreting situations in ways that lead to negative, counterproductive emotions, we can interpret situations in ways that lead to positive, productive emotions — one of which is gratitude.

No matter your circumstances, you can always choose to view your current circumstances gratefully (e.g., I'm grateful for the new assignment at work, because it gives me the opportunity to demonstrate my knowledge and proficiency). You can choose to focus on the positive future outcomes of your current situation (e.g., I'm grateful that the universe is impermanent, because it means I always have opportunities for second chances and to learn from and improve upon my mistakes.) And, you can choose to focus on how much better your current situation is than it could be (e.g., I'm grateful, because at least the car's not totaled.)

Today, pause now and then to cultivate a feeling of gratitude by not only thinking about something you are grateful for, but holding that thing in mind and really focusing all of your attention on what it is and why you are grateful for it. If you do this exercise while experiencing a negative emotion, notice how quickly that negative emotion goes away. Notice how your thoughts have completely changed and are now eliciting more peaceful and serene feelings in both your body and mind.

35

Built-In Virtual Reality

"Imagination is everything. It is the preview of life's coming attractions." – Albert Einstein

Our brains are mighty virtual reality machines, and we can use that fact to help us develop in myriad ways.

Any time we want, we can create vivid, realistic experiences in our minds. I say "experiences" rather than "images", because what we create can be so much more than simply a visual image. We can create or recreate complete experiences that include any or all of the five senses as well as emotions. How can we use this ability in helpful ways?

When we create clear, vivid experiences in our minds, we activate neural pathways. Each time we activate the same, or very similar pathways, we enhance the efficiency of the neural connections made along that pathway. This is a concept known as neuroplasticity. When we use our minds to create experiences that mimic reality as perfectly as possible, including all relevant sensory and emotional components, we activate neural pathways in the same way they would be activated out in the real world.

Therefore, we can imagine various scenarios in ways that improve how we handle those circumstances when we encounter them in real life.

For example, we can rehearse physical tasks we might be trying to learn (e.g., juggling, shooting); boost motivation by seeing ourselves successfully completing a goal (e.g., getting a degree); enhance confidence by seeing ourselves overcoming challenges we are worried about (e.g., maintaining a healthy diet during the holidays); and practice managing a variety of emotions (e.g., nervousness, fear, anger).

Today, think about things you'd like to get better at. Maybe it's a skill you're trying to improve, having challenging conversations with your spouse, or staying motivated to get done what you know needs to be done. Then, take some time to engage in mental imagery. Vividly and realistically imagine the scenario you identified and experience yourself navigating that situation in a productive, successful way.

36

Life Is Happening Now...Only Now

"The only thing that is ultimately real about your journey is the step that you are taking at this moment. That's all there ever is."
– Eckhart Tolle

Life occurs in the present moment. We can remember the past and anticipate the future, but right now, this moment, is the only moment that truly exists.

This is critical information to remember for at least two reasons. First, the present moment is the only moment you can truly experience. The past and future are only stories. In the present, however, we experience reality in ways that simply aren't possible via memory or imagination. Second, the future is created by what we do in the present moment. Every perception, feeling, choice, and behavior that occurs in the present moment will color and influence the future. In the Here and Now is where we create not only our physical realities but our psychological and emotional realities as well.

Today, deliberately pause every so often to recognize where your attention is. Notice if you are lost in thought about the past or future. Notice if you are carrying on imaginary conversations with others or yourself. In these moments when you recognize that you are not in the present moment, take a breath and really tune into your physical surroundings. What do you see, hear, and smell? What does the floor or chair feel like underneath you? Once you've taken a moment to attend fully to your physical surroundings, turn your attention inward. What are you feeling physically (e.g., tired, sore)? What are you feeling emotionally (e.g., anxious, content)?

It's amazing how little time we are truly tuned into our present internal and external environments, particularly given the fact that this present moment, right now, is the only moment in which reality actually exists.

37

Embrace Change

*"Some changes look negative on the surface but you will soon realize
that space is being created in your life for something new to emerge."*
– Eckhart Tolle

If there is one constant in this universe, it's change.

Change is inevitable and occurs all the time. Our bodies
are changing day by day, hour by hour, even second by second.
Our understanding of ourselves, the world, and those around us
changes with every new thought, encounter, and experience we
have. Like it or not, nothing is permanent.

Sometimes we view change as good. We often hope for and
welcome change and are grateful for change when it happens.
Other times, however, we view change as bad and highly stressful,
especially when that change is accompanied by uncertainty and a
lack of control.

Today, think about all the change that is currently happening to
you or around you. That change may be expected or unexpected,
happening quickly or slowly, or in or out of your control. Regardless

of the type of change that is happening, see if you can think about that change as a normal and natural part of life and accept your situation as it is right now, in the present moment.

Then, think about that change in a helpful way, a way that generates positive emotion and allows you to deal with that change in productive ways. For example, the change you might notice is more pounds gathering around your middle than you're comfortable with. You can view that change as a good thing, because it has clued you into the fact that you have gotten lazy with your nutrition and exercise regimen. Or, maybe you're noticing your kids needing you less and less as they get older. That change might be good, because it allows you to spend less time supervising your kids and more time engaging in hobbies or activities that you were forced to put to the side while your kids were young and required more attention.

Whatever your current situation, change is a part of it...and will remain a part of it for the rest of your life. That's just fact. And fighting against change, trying to push back against the reality of impermanence, is a lot like trying to sweep the sand off the beach...a Sisyphean task. Embrace change and find comfort in impermanence. After all, growth, development, and improvement would all be impossible if "permanent" was a real thing.

38

Attention – Where Is Your Spotlight?

"Control of consciousness determines the quality of life." – Mihaly Csikszentmihalyi

D r. Amishi Jha described our attentional focus in terms of a spotlight. Whatever our spotlight is pointed at, that is what we experience in our conscious awareness. Our spotlights can be wide or narrow and focused on things inside ourselves (e.g., thoughts, emotions, physiology) or outside ourselves. The important thing to remember is that only what falls within our spotlight is what enters our consciousness.

Where is your spotlight focused? Is your spotlight pointed inside yourself, illuminating memories of the past or stories about the future? Or, is your spotlight focused on aspects of your current environment, in the here and now, in the present moment? There are times when thinking about the past or future can be helpful, useful things to do. However, reality exists only in the here and now and will only be truly experienced and remembered if your attention is focused on it.

So, today, notice where your spotlight is pointed, and challenge yourself to keep it focused on things that matter in the here and now, the things that help you be at your best in the present moment. Distractions are inevitable, as is "mental time-travel" to the past or future. When you notice those distractions, though, deliberately refocus your spotlight on whatever it is in your current situation that is important. In this way, you will not only experience more of reality; you will create memories that will last throughout your life.

39

Impulsivity – Are You Reacting or Responding?

"Respond; Don't react. Listen; Don't talk. Think; Don't assume." Raji Lukkoor

Have you ever been in a situation where something happened, and you reacted immediately in a way that you later regretted? Maybe you learned information later that you didn't have in the moment, and that information completely changed how you understood the event. Or, after taking time to allow emotions to dissipate, you realized that you misunderstood the intentions or severity of the event that occurred.

Often when things happen to us, we react almost automatically. These reactions are based on our initial, heat-of-the-moment interpretations of the events we experience. In a split second, we assign meaning to someone's words or actions and then react based on that meaning without ever pausing to double-check that our perception was actually correct.

Today, when events or interactions with other people drive an immediate emotional reaction, take a moment to pause and reflect more deeply on the situation. Take the time necessary to examine the situation from multiple angles. Seek out information that is not immediately apparent in that first moment. In this way, you can ensure that your understanding of the situation is thorough. As a result, you will be able to respond rather than react. You will be able to take helpful, productive action based on accurate information rather than counterproductive, impulsive action based on partial, limited information.

40

Goals – Be Patient and Embrace Challenge

"Be practical as well as generous in your ideals. Keep your eyes on the stars, but remember to keep your feet on the ground." – Theodore Roosevelt

The goals we set don't happen overnight, nor does our progress occur in a linear fashion…and we need to remember that.

When we regularly pursue goals, those end states we've identified are consistently in the forefront of our minds. We think about them in the shower, while working out, at work, and (too many times) when we're trying to sleep. Keeping our goals and, more importantly, the reasons we want to achieve those goals regularly in our awareness is a good thing; however, we need to temper our vision and excitement with some realism.

Goal progress rarely occurs in a predictable, linear way. For every three steps we take forward, we may take one or two steps back. Life's challenges…some anticipated, many not…regularly affect our ability to stick to our goal plan and, therefore, the progress we are realistically able to make. Recognizing and accepting this as a normal part of goal pursuit can reduce the stress, anxiety, frustration, and guilt associated with failing to achieve daily or weekly objectives and make it easier to re-evaluate and reorganize our plans in a way that accommodates our new realities.

Today, think about the goals you've set and achieved in the past. Did you achieve those goals immediately? With no unexpected challenges or deviations from the initial timeline and plan you developed? Probably not. So, accept that the current goals you have for yourself will be no different. Be patient, and embrace both the long-term nature of the goal and the challenges you'll encounter during its pursuit. Both make the ultimate achievement of the goal more satisfying...and inevitably result in some outstanding stories about the whole process!

41

Impermanence – Every Situation is Different

"No man ever steps in the same river twice, for it's not the same river and he's not the same man."– Heraclitus

Have you ever looked at the caller ID on your phone… heard your child say, "Hey Mom/Dad! Can you come here?"…or walked into the regularly scheduled weekly meeting at work and thought, "Here we go again…"?

Because we are built to adapt, remember, and learn from our past, it is easy to go into situations expecting them to be similar to, or even exactly like, situations we've experienced before. However, life doesn't work that way. No situation is exactly the same as any other situation for any number of reasons, but the most important and consistent reason is YOU.

Even if nothing else changed, YOU are different. You might be in a different mood or have had more or less sleep, but without a doubt, you've experienced more things going into this situation than you had when you went into seemingly similar situations in the past. You have the benefit of hindsight, and as a result, you have the ability to think and act in ways that will affect your experience this time around.

So, as you encounter moments throughout your day when you think, "Here we go again", think about how things went last time and how a simple change in attitude, thought process, or behavior on your part might make things go very differently, and hopefully better, this time around.

42

Question Your Perceptions

"What we observe is not nature itself, but nature exposed to our method of questioning." – Werner Heisenberg

Every minute of every day, we move through a world that we can only perceive a tiny percentage of. We are limited physically by the range and sensitivity of our five senses and mentally by our knowledge, past experiences, values, and beliefs. Because of these limitations, it behooves us to always double-check our perceptions, particularly in situations in which how we perceive things will influence truly consequential behavior.

Today, any time you notice any feelings of irritation or frustration, pause and ask yourself why you are frustrated. Chances are, it's because you believe somebody or something is treating you unfairly or harming you in some way. Once you identify the perception that is the source of your anger, irritation, or frustration, question that perception. Ask yourself if there are any other ways that you might be able to understand the situation. Ask yourself if there are other ways that the situation could be viewed besides how you currently view it. Ask yourself if there is any information you're assuming or conclusions you're drawing, not based on what you are actually experiencing, but on past experiences you've had in similar situations.

Questioning your perceptions in these ways will help ensure that your understanding of your circumstances is as accurate and thorough as it can be, which, ultimately, will help you to choose the most productive ways to handle whatever your circumstances might be.

43

Good News – How Do You Respond When Someone Shares It With You?

"To get the full value of joy, you must have someone to divide it with."
– Mark Twain

Building and maintaining connections with others can be challenging; however, creating and sustaining relationships is essential for our overall well-being.

When we care about people, we want to be there for them when things go wrong. If one of our friends or family members is going through a rough time, we immediately speak up and ask if there is anything we can do. We might even take it upon ourselves to assess the situation and do something we think might bring them joy (e.g., sending flowers) or make their lives a little easier (e.g., taking them a prepared meal). Connecting with those important to us when things go wrong is important…but what about when things go right? How do we respond when people are excited about something good that happened in their lives and want to share that news with us?

How we respond when people choose us to share good news with is just as important as how we respond when they share bad news. There are really only four ways to respond when someone shares good news with us. Three of those ways will worsen the relationship we have with that person, and one of those ways will build the relationship we have with that person. None of the ways will allow our relationship to remain as it was before they shared the good news.

When someone shares good news with you, you can 1) be somewhat engaged, not ignoring but not really attending to them either, 2) change the topic of conversation to you by either disregarding what they've said altogether or by "one-upping" them with something from your life you think is in the same vein as, but better than, what they brought up, 3) point out all of the things wrong with the situation they're describing, all the ways you think the good news they're sharing isn't really good, or 4) fully engage with that individual by actively listening, asking questions about their news that allow them to describe in even more detail what happened and why they're happy about it. Only the fourth type of response will build your relationship with that person; the other three responses will deteriorate your relationship over time.

Today, notice when someone chooses you to share good news with, keep these four possible response styles in mind, and be conscious of how you respond in that moment. If you find yourself falling into one of the response styles that will deteriorate the relationship, adjust. Shift your focus directly to the individual, engage fully with eye contact and body language, and ask that person to elaborate on the news. Encourage them to talk a little bit more and in a little more detail about whatever it was that brought them joy. Both you and the other person will benefit individually, and you can be certain that you have taken a small step toward a stronger, more solid relationship with this person you care about.

44

Acceptance – Lack of Control

"Accept that things happen. It may not be for a reason, and you may have no control over it, but the first step to getting through it is accepting what it is." – Kurt Vonnegut

Regardless of whether you believe the universe is random or deterministic, things happen in our lives that we can't do anything about. In those situations, acceptance is the only option.

Some people believe that everything happens randomly with no rhyme nor reason. Other people believe that everything happens as a direct result of something that happened or the will of a deity. Still others don't care, fall somewhere in the middle, or simply choose to spend their time thinking about more tangible, real-world issues. Regardless of which category you fall into, you encounter situations every day that you can't change. Things happen in your life that you can do nothing about.

When we find ourselves experiencing things we can't control, we really only have two choices, accept our circumstances and deal with the ramifications of the situation as best we can or drive ourselves crazy with thoughts that begin with "What if I'd…" or "If only I'd…". The sooner we recognize and accept the reality that the situation is how it is, and no amount of wishing can change it, we can begin thinking proactively about handling the situation as productively as possible.

Acceptance doesn't mean we've resigned ourselves to whatever fate has dropped in our laps. It simply gives us a starting point, in the here and now, from which to begin to affect change…even if the only thing we can change about the situation is how we choose to think about and react to it.

Today, when you find yourself affected by something you can't control, take a minute to simply accept what is. If those "What if" thoughts arise, let them go and simply focus on what your reality is now, in the present moment. Then, accept that reality, choose how you want to perceive and react to that reality, and progress with life as productively as you can.

45

Cognitive Dissonance – Are You Doing What You Think You Should Be Doing?

"So far, about morals, I know only that what is moral is what you feel good after and what is immoral is what you feel bad after." – Ernest Hemingway

When your behaviors align with your values, we avoid a lot of discomfort in our lives.

Cognitive dissonance is the unpleasant feeling we have when we act in ways that we believe we should not be acting. Usually, we experience cognitive dissonance when our behaviors don't match up with the things we say we value and care about. For example, imagine you value your health and know that smoking can endanger it, but you smoke a cigarette anyway. While smoking that cigarette, you will experience cognitive dissonance.

When we experience cognitive dissonance, there are only three ways to get rid of it. We can change the behavior, change the belief, or rationalize the behavior in some way. In the example above, the first way you could eliminate cognitive dissonance is to stop smoking the cigarette. The second way to eliminate cognitive dissonance is to stop caring about your health. The final way to possibly eliminate, but more likely only reduce, cognitive dissonance is to create an excuse for smoking (e.g., I'm really stressed, and it's only one).

Rather than being reactive and trying to deal with cognitive dissonance when it arises, it behooves us to avoid it altogether. And the best way to do that is to ensure your behaviors align with your values. That is, make sure that your choices, words, and actions represent the values you care about, the things that truly matter to you.

Today, remind yourself regularly of your values and how you want to be as you live life and interact with others. Also, immediately tune into any discomfort you feel when you act or speak in a certain way and ask yourself if those feelings might be cognitive dissonance. Ask yourself if your actions and behaviors in that moment align with your values. If you approach your day with this deliberate and intentional awareness, you can increase the consistency with which your actions align with the things that matter to you and avoid the discomfort and guilt associated with cognitive dissonance.

46

Turning Around Bad Moods

"When you arise in the morning, give thanks for the food and for the joy of living. If you see no reason for giving thanks, the fault lies only in yourself." – Tecumseh

All of us have days when we find ourselves in a bad mood. Maybe it's a lack of sleep or some last-minute obligations. Maybe it's a feeling of being completely overwhelmed by life or continually bombarded with incessant minor annoyances. Whatever it is that's going on, though, the mood that we're in causes us to view everything happening to us as bad.

Although these moods can be challenging to shake, eliciting a feeling of gratitude for your present situation is one of the best ways to boost your mood in these situations. Here are a couple of suggestions for cultivating gratitude, even for life's most challenging circumstances.

Notice or think about somebody whose life is far more challenging than yours. That person might be in a different country or standing next to you on a corner asking for change. But wherever that person is, bringing to mind somebody dealing with a situation far worse than you can help change your perspective of what's going on in your life to one of gratitude rather than annoyance.

Also, you can think about how much worse things could be than what they are. For example, if you're sitting in traffic or seem to be hitting every red light on a road, imagine if, instead, you were sitting on the side of the road with a car that was broken down. Or, if you're sitting on the side of road next to a broken down car, imagine if you'd just been in a wreck and were injured while sitting next to a car that had been totaled. Keeping in mind that things can always be worse can, again, shift your perspective from one of irritation to one of gratitude.

Today, if you find yourself falling into a negative, pessimistic outlook on life, deliberately cultivate gratitude by stepping outside your circumstances to imagine how much worse others' situations are or how much worse your current situation could be than what it actually is. I think you'll be surprised at quickly your mood will change for the better.

47

Create Good Habits

"Every habit and capability is confirmed and grows in its corresponding actions, walking by walking, and running by running... Therefore, if you want to do something, make a habit of it, if you don't want to do that, don't, but make a habit of something else instead." – Epictetus

How can we help ensure that our behaviors are ones we want, those that are helpful and in line with our core values and beliefs? Make those behaviors habits.

As humans, we are excellent at creating habits. When we pay little to no attention to our behaviors and simply react to momentary thoughts or impulses, the habits we inevitably create can be ones we wish we didn't have. However, we can also choose our habits more strategically. When we identify behaviors that we want to sustain (e.g., exercising, meditating, reading), create a schedule for when they will happen, and deliberately engage in these desired behaviors...good habits are born.

Today, think about what behaviors you'd like to make habits. What do you believe you should be doing more often or more regularly than you currently are? Whatever these behaviors are, decide when you're going to do them. Adopt techniques that will remind you they need to be done. Create environments that make the behaviors as easy as possible (e.g., exercise clothes set out next to the bed; healthy lunch packed the night before). And create strategies that help you keep in mind the reason why these behaviors are important, how these behaviors align with your values, the things that truly matter to you, the way you want to live your life.

Finally, heed Epictetus's advice from the quote above…engage in the behaviors over and over and over again. Your human brain will take care of the rest, and before you know it, your desired habit will be born.

48

Identifying Invisible Values

When thinking about your personal values, it might be fairly easy to identify values you think are important for yourself as well as the corresponding behaviors aligned with those values (e.g., "People should always try their best no matter what. So, I will give my full effort in every endeavor I undertake."). However, what about values you've internalized that you don't even know about? What if your behavior is being driven by these values (and it is) in ways you aren't aware of? What if those ways don't match up with your consciously chosen values?

Think about the culture you live in. How many mores do you adhere to each day? Mores are unwritten rules, things that "go without saying", cultural norms so embedded within our psyche that we don't even notice them. For example, I imagine you don't cut in line, because you know it's wrong. But where is that written? The answer is that it's not written, but you still know that cutting in line is wrong. So, you (probably) don't do it. Examples of mores abound within all cultures be they cultures created by families, organizations, or geographic locations.

Today, try to recognize the mores that are driving your behaviors

Notice how easily and without thought you navigate yourself to the right side of the sidewalk or hallway (if in the U.S.). Notice your tendency to allow others to complete a thought before you offer your opinions (hopefully!). Notice how people in an elevator naturally move backward to let others onto the elevator. Notice all those behaviors occurring around you and in which you are engaged that follow clearly defined and well-understood rules that aren't written down anywhere.

While bringing into your awareness these cultural norms that "go without saying", try to identify mores that don't align with the values you hold. For example, maybe one of your core values is that people should show kindness by helping other people. However, one of the mores within your work culture is that people should work independently and take care of their own problems. How do you feel when you see a coworker struggling? What do you do? What do you want to do? If what you want to do isn't what you actually do, why don't you act differently?

Values, both personally chosen and culturally adopted, drive our attention, thinking, and choices every day. The more aware we are of these values, the more able we are to think and behave in ways that are deliberate and consciously chosen instead of impulsive and reactive.

49

What Does Realistic Mean?

"The greatest danger for most of us is not that our aim is too high and we miss it, but that it is too low and we reach it." Michelangelo

There's a popular acronym that describes five qualities that many authors have asserted goals should have: SMART – Specific, Measurable, Action-Focused, *Realistic,* Time-bound. But how do we know if something is realistic? How do we know whether it's realistic to expect to attain a goal we haven't tried yet to attain?

Some will say that, as human beings, we are self-aware and have the benefit of not only past experience but also knowledge of our inner selves…our personalities, energy levels, resilience, confidence, motivation, etc. Using this knowledge, these people say, allows us to accurately predict what achievements are realistic for us to expect to accomplish. This approach sounds rational; however, consider this....

Imagine that you see potential in someone you really care about. It might be a child, spouse, friend, employee, or coworker. You believe that this person can achieve a certain goal; let's say it's to get a college degree. That person, though, does NOT believe that they are capable of getting a college degree, and they cite all kinds of reasons why they can't achieve that goal. They tell you about their busy schedule, their learning disability, their ADHD, their lack of skill in reading or writing...they tell you all kinds of reasons why there is no way that getting a college degree is a *reasonable* goal for them to set. You, however, believe differently.

You don't discount the fact that there will be obstacles along the way, maybe even the exact obstacles articulated by the individual. But you have had enough experience with this individual to believe very strongly that they have what it takes to overcome the inevitable challenges they will face on the way to getting a college degree. So, you persuade that person to give it a shot and let them know that you will be there to support them every step of the way. The person agrees and begins the degree program. Sure enough, that person faces myriad challenges, but sure enough...as you expected...that person has the wherewithal to overcome each of those challenges and, ultimately, gets the college degree.

Unfortunately, we often are bad judges of how realistic something is for us. We may, for a variety of reasons, doubt our abilities. People who know us well, however, may see things differently. What we consider to be unreasonable, they see as not only reasonable but a fantastic opportunity for growth and development.

Today, if there is a goal that you are thinking about, but you haven't committed to pursuing that goal because you don't know if the goal is reasonable, I encourage you to consult with someone who knows you well and has your best interests at heart...someone you trust. Ask this person what they think about how reasonable your goal pursuit is. If they tell you they think that you are capable of doing something you don't believe you can, ask them why they believe that and listen to their reasoning with an open mind. Then, take a chance and trust their judgment.

You might be surprised at what is really realistic *for you.*

50

Identifying Values and Beliefs

External circumstances don't determine how we feel or what we do. The ways we perceive those circumstances are what determine how we feel and what we do. Furthermore, our perceptions, the meaning that we assign to our circumstances, are determined to a large extent by our beliefs and values. Therefore, because of the significant influence beliefs and values have on how we understand reality, it behooves us to have a thorough understanding of what our values and beliefs are.

If we put some time and effort into identifying our core values and beliefs, chances are we'll be able to come up with some of those values and beliefs very easily. However, other values and beliefs, although regularly present and strongly affecting our perceptions, may be more challenging for us to identify. Two ways that we can go about trying to pinpoint some of those values and beliefs that may be more difficult to recognize are journaling and tuning into emotional reactions in the moment.

When we take the time to write in a journal, we process information differently than when we just ponder that information in our minds. We're able to take a broader, more analytical perspective that's not possible when we are currently entangled in a situation. When examining your values and beliefs through journaling, ask and answer questions like: "Why do I care so much about achieving this particular goal. In fact, why did I choose this thing as a goal in the first place?", "Why is it that I get so worked up around this one person?", and "What is it about this situation that made/makes me anxious/nervous/excited/frustrated every time I encounter it?" Answering these questions with the natural distance created by the journaling process can help you identify some values/beliefs that may influence you in ways you weren't previously aware of.

We can also identify values/beliefs in the moment. As soon as you notice yourself experiencing a strong emotional reaction, regardless of what the emotion is, ask yourself why. Why do you feel so strongly? What aspect of the situation are you paying the most attention to? What is it about the situation that really matters to you? Why do you care so much? By recognizing strong emotions as soon as they arise and then questioning why those emotions arose…where they came from…we can gain valuable insight into the values/beliefs that may be driving our perceptions and experiences in that moment.

51

What Role Are You Playing in Others' Stories?

"The task is...not so much to see what no one has yet seen; but to think what nobody has yet thought, about that which everybody sees." –
Erwin Schrödinger

Most of the time we walk through the world examining our environment and interactions with others from our own points of view. We evaluate our circumstances solely in terms of how others and things affect us, the role that those things and people are playing in our lives. However, being able to step outside our own limited perspectives and see things from different angles and through others' eyes is essential if we want to 1) ensure that we have an accurate and thorough understanding of what is going on and 2) empathize and connect with other people as best we can.

As you walk through your day, notice when you are caught in the creation and living out of your own story, and then change your perspective. Instead of focusing only the role that people, things, and circumstances are playing in your life, consider what role you are playing in their lives. This can be a fun exercise because you don't have to limit yourself to reality. Learning to see things from perspectives other than our own is a skill and can be practiced with anything. For example, considering the role you're playing in your friend's life in a particular moment is certainly helpful and may allow you connect better with that friend. But, considering the role you're playing in the life of your pet or your car or your clothes can be useful, too. Not only is considering "life" from the perspective of those things creative and fun, it will help you to develop the skill of stepping outside your own point of view…and that's really the goal.

So, today, consider the story that other people or things would tell about you. How are you seen and understood by others? Considering life from these alternative perspectives can help build the skill of mental agility and may even lead to personal insights about yourself and the world around you that you may never have otherwise been aware of.

52

Gaining Perspective – The 30,000 ft View

"The only people who see the whole picture are the ones who step outside the frame." – Salman Rushdie

Most of us live busy lives with various things we have to manage happening all the time. In this type of hectic environment, it's easy to get overwhelmed by the sheer number of responsibilities, seemingly all needing to be tended to simultaneously. In these situations, it can be helpful to take a step back and remind ourselves of the bigger picture.

Today, if you find yourself feeling stressed out or overwhelmed, distance yourself from your immediate situation. Take a moment to imagine how important what you're worrying about will be a year from now. Does this moment generating all of this stress truly matter in the grand scheme of things? Are your actions and decisions right now going to determine your future? Your kids' futures? The future of all humankind? Probably not. Gaining perspective in this way can remove a lot of pressure and immediately reduce the stress you feel. You will be amazed at how quickly you are again able to think and act productively.

The choices we make in the present moment absolutely affect our futures. However, those choices are rarely as big and important as we sometimes allow our minds to make them. So, step back, take a breath, see the big picture, and recognize that your circumstances…regardless of what they are…are manageable. Make sure you consider the entire forest rather than just the trees surrounding you…step outside the frame.

53

Habit Energy – Turn Off the Autopilot

"Habit energy is pushing us; it pushes us to do things without our being aware. Sometimes we do something without knowing we're doing it. Even when we don't want to do something, we still do it…. With awareness, we have a choice; we can act another way." – Thich Nhat Hahn

Too often, our brains operate on autopilot. We interact with the world in rote, habitual ways without really stopping to think about what we're doing or why we're doing it. We fail to consider whether what we're doing is really the best thing for us and those around us. We react impulsively to the various stimuli we encounter without stopping to reflect on whether our actions are appropriate or whether we even understand the situation accurately in the first place.

Today, notice those moments when you are operating on autopilot. When you catch yourself meandering through life in this manner, take a second to pause and think about what you are doing and why you're doing it. If something happens, and you have a knee-jerk response…either behaviorally or verbally…notice that impulsive, habitual response and question where it came from. Ask yourself why you reacted that way. Delve more deeply into the nature of your circumstances. Is the way you are interpreting things…your perception of the situation…accurate? Is there another way to see the situation? Might there be information about what's going on that you don't currently have?

Asking and answering these questions can break us out of that reactive, autopilot mode and help ensure that we are speaking and acting in the most productive ways and accurately and thoroughly understanding the cornucopia of events we engage in every day.

54

Habits Are More Than Just What You Do

"Such as are your habitual thoughts, such also will be the character of your mind; for the soul is dyed by the thoughts." – Marcus Aurelius

When we think of habits, most of us think about behaviors that we do without thinking. We think of actions so ingrained within us that we do them unconsciously. However, habits aren't limited to behaviors; we develop thought and emotional habits as well.

For example, what is the first thing you think when your alarm goes off in the morning? Is it the same every day? Is there someone you can think of who immediately elicits the same emotions every time you're around them? These emotions might be positive (e.g., joy, comfort) or negative (e.g., fear, irritation), but they are consistently and automatically felt every time you encounter…or even think about…this person. Is there a place you go that produces predictable thoughts and feelings even as soon as you park your car? For example, whenever you pull into the parking lot at your job you might think, "Here we go again," and feel frustration, nervousness, excitement, joy, or irritation.

In all of these cases, we have developed habitual thoughts that automatically drive predictable emotions. We have become so accustomed to interpreting our environments, situations, and interactions in certain ways that those interpretations have become a knee-jerk, reactionary response. We don't choose this response based on our awareness of our unique circumstances. Instead, our minds immediately latch onto the thoughts we always have when faced with those same conditions.

Today, notice those times when thoughts come into your head automatically and ask yourself whether or not these same thoughts are present every time you encounter that situation. For example, is there a specific thought or emotion you experience whenever you are stopped by a red light? Or when you are forced to stand in a long line? Or when it's time to pack up and go home from work? Recognize those thoughts and emotions that show up automatically.

Habits...whether they are behaviors, thoughts, or emotions... can be helpful and productive or harmful and counterproductive. However, regardless of the type, we can extinguish or create habits at will. It simply takes conscious awareness, deliberate effort, and time.

55

Basic Psychological Needs – Autonomy

"Find out who you are and do it on purpose." – Dolly Parton

There are three psychological needs that are basic and necessary for all human beings. These needs are autonomy, competence, and relatedness. Each of these needs is satisfied only to the extent we believe they are. That is, if we believe that we are acting without feeling pressured, competent or capable of being competent, and connected to and valued by other people, then our three basic psychological needs are satisfied. Because there are three needs, we will describe the needs one at a time and then focus on some ways to help ensure that these needs are met throughout your day.

The need of autonomy refers to our need to feel like our actions are undertaken of our own accord, of our volition. When the need for autonomy is met, we do not feel pressured to do what we're doing, and we understand both the relevance and significance of our actions. The need for autonomy is most likely to be satisfied when our behaviors align with our core values and beliefs. In other words, what we are actually doing is something we believe we should be doing…something important that needs to be done.

Today, when you're running an errand, doing something for work, or just engaging in some everyday life activity, check in to see whether you feel like you have to do this thing or are being forced to do this thing. Also, ask yourself why you're doing what you're doing. Is it simply to obtain some outcome you want or avoid some outcome you don't want? Or, is it because you see the value and importance of what you're doing, because you believe that what you're doing is significant for its own sake?

To enhance the likelihood of satisfying our need for autonomy we need to make sure that our actions are aligned with our values and that we understand and agree with the reasons and rationale for what we're doing. When this is the case, we don't feel like we are being pressured or forced in any way. We do what we do simply because we believe it's right.

56

Competence

"If you can do a half-assed job of anything, you're a one-eyed man in a kingdom of the blind." – Kurt Vonnegut

Another basic psychological need is competence. Our need for competence is satisfied when we believe that we are capable of being effective at whatever it is we're doing. We don't have to believe we're currently good at something; we simply need to believe that we can become good at something. We need to believe that we can move the needle a meaningful amount in the right direction.

When we talk about competence, it obviously begs the question, competence concerning what? The answer is, anything…anything from making a cup of coffee to being a human being. Anything that you can think of in terms of whether you are good at it or not is something that can affect the satisfaction of your need for competence.

Because the need for competence is satisfied only when we believe it is satisfied, our perceptions and how we choose to explain and understand our circumstances and abilities determine whether or not our need for competence is met. This is good news because we are in control of our thoughts and perceptions and can, therefore, adjust our perceptions in ways that boost the likelihood that our need for competence will be satisfied.

Unfortunately, though, for the same reason (i.e., because competence depends on individual perceptions), we can't change other people's perceived competence levels. We can, however, do things that will make it more likely that people's need for competence is satisfied. For example, if you are a leader (e.g., boss, coach, parent), you can ensure that the people you lead are, as often as possible, engaged in tasks that are challenging but not too challenging…tasks they will be able to do with maximal effort and possibly a little bit of help or guidance from you. Also, when you provide feedback in the form of either criticism or praise, you can focus that feedback on things the person can control, things they can either repeat in the future if the person was successful or things they can change in order to improve the outcome the next time around.

Today, check in with yourself every now and then, and ask yourself, "Am I effective, or capable of being effective, at….?" If the answer is no, look for different ways to view your situation. Identify strengths you have and aren't bringing to the table or strengths you are bringing to the table and just don't realize it. Often, we pay a lot more attention to our weaknesses than our strengths, so our strengths and the contributions we make normally, naturally, and consistently throughout our day can easily go unnoticed. Also, if you are a leader, pay attention to those you lead and evaluate the extent to which they believe they are capable of being effective. Be cognizant of the difficulty levels of the tasks you assign, the content and focus of the feedback you provide, and the manner in which that feedback is provided.

57

Relatedness

"We don't accomplish anything in this world alone...and whatever happens is the result of the whole tapestry of one's life and the weaving of individual threads from one to another that creates something." – Sandra Day O'Connor

The final basic psychological need is relatedness. The need for relatedness is satisfied when we believe that we are an important and valued member of a group. That is, when we believe that we are an accepted and integral part of a group, not only for what we produce or bring to the table but for ourselves as individuals, our need for relatedness is likely to be satisfied.

Again, because our basic psychological needs are only satisfied if we believe them to be, it is important to build and maintain an awareness of our perceptions. If we find ourselves in a situation in which we don't believe that our need for relatedness is being satisfied, we should first question our perceptions. We should ask ourselves whether the way we understand others' motives and behaviors is accurate. We should ask ourselves if our perceptions about our relationships and connections with others are accurate. Sometimes, simply by giving people the benefit of the doubt, we realize that our relationships with those individuals are not as tenuous, strained, or contentious as we'd originally thought.

When serving as leaders trying to set conditions for others' need for relatedness to be satisfied, we can do our best to create as open, accepting, and nonjudgmental an environment as possible. We can emphasize compassion, actively listen, and do our best to empathize with others…to see situations through their eyes and understand things from their points of view.

Today, notice those environments in which you truly feel like an accepted and valued member of a group. Notice, too, any situations when you might not feel like you are valued, accepted, and important…times when you feel like you're on the outside looking in, or even actively being ostracized by others. Then, compare those two very different perceptions in terms of your feelings, attitudes, mindsets, and behaviors.

58

What Are You Worried About?

"How much pain have cost us the evils which have never happened?"
– Thomas Jefferson

"We suffer more often in imagination than reality." – Seneca

Worry, fear, anxiety, nervousness. What these emotions have in common is that they are 1) everyday feelings commonly experienced by all human beings and 2) driven by things that are not real.

When we are worried or nervous, we are worried or nervous about something…something that, by definition, hasn't happened. We are nervous about what we think might happen. We are worried about what we think might take place.

Although planning for contingencies can be a productive thing to do, allowing ourselves to become immersed in thoughts about potential problems is not productive at all. Worry requires that our attention be placed on the future rather than the present moment and demands a great deal of mental, physical, and emotional energy…and for what purpose? How many times have you worried about something that never happened? Or, worried about something that did happen but wasn't nearly as bad as you'd anticipated in your mind?

Today, recognize those moments when you feel worried or nervous. Notice that your attention is not on anything actually happening but on what you believe could happen in the future. The future is created by our actions in the present. If you're worried about something in the future, take steps now, in the present moment, to eliminate…or at least mitigate…whatever it is you're worried about. It is amazing how quickly worry disappears once action is initiated.

This is only possible, however, if you have some semblance of control over the situation…and often we don't. This lack of control isn't a problem, though. It's a free pass to a worry-free present. If there's nothing you can do about the situation, then there is no need to think about it. What will happen, will happen, and you will deal with what occurs when it becomes necessary for you to deal with it. Let go of the future, of trying to control something you can't control, and come back to the present moment…the only moment where reality actually exists.

59

Close the Deal

"The illusion that we understand the past fosters overconfidence in our ability to predict the future." – Daniel Kahneman

Have you ever begun and made good progress on a project or goal only to ultimately have that project fail or goal fall by the wayside? Was it because somewhere along the way you became complacent, believing that you were doing perfectly well and that success was inevitable, only to have things fall apart, apparently overnight and out of nowhere? Two reasons this complacency might develop are: overconfidence and habit.

When we begin pursuing something new, we are often excited and energetic, and that excitement and energy lead to a lot of progress at the beginning of our pursuit. Having experienced success quickly and…seemingly…easily, we can become overconfident. We can begin to believe that the rest of what we need to do to achieve success will come as easily and with as few challenges as what we've already done. This overconfidence can lull us into a sense of complacency that can stop our progress in its tracks.

Habit can also contribute to complacency. Habit, when it comes to a new life pursuit, can be extremely helpful. Creating habits that move you closer to your goal in consistent ways and at predictable times is an excellent way to help ensure that life's unavoidable challenges don't distract your attention away from what you need to do to achieve what you've set out to achieve. However, because of the ever-changing nature of life and the fact that different phases of goal pursuit require different behaviors, habits…even ones that were productive at one point…can become counterproductive. Maybe you developed a habit that helped you stick to a plan of action necessary for progress in one phase of your goal, but the next phase of your goal requires a different plan of action not at all supported but, in fact, hindered by your current habit.

Each of these issues related to complacency, overconfidence, and habit can be minimized by keeping your attention focused on the present moment. Staying focused on what is required right now for success can help you undo the power of counterproductive habits. And, letting go of whatever successes or failures you've experienced in the past and focusing, instead, on what is necessary right now can help reduce or eliminate overconfidence.

60

Just Do It

"Many strokes, though with a little axe, hew down and fell the hardest-timber'd oak." – William Shakespeare

"A tree thick enough to embrace grows from the tiny sapling. A tower of nine levels starts from the dirt heap. A journey of a thousand miles begins beneath the feet." – Lao Tzu, Tao de Ching

Getting started can be hard.

When we set a new goal, it's useful to think through what we're going to need in order to achieve that goal. Brainstorming and gathering knowledge from people can be helpful; identifying resources you'll need is critical, and planning not only for what you need to do but for what you need to avoid is essential. However, after all of the identifying and planning and talking comes the doing…and that's where a lot of people get stuck.

We have patterns and habits that we have adopted and that guide most of our behaviors and interactions throughout the day. However, like Thomas Jefferson (and many others) said, "If you want something you've never had, you have to do something you've never done." This requires us to fight inertia, break out of those patterns and habits, and adopt new behaviors that will help us achieve our goal. Sometimes, too, the sheer volume of things we need to do to pursue our goals is overwhelming. There are just so many things in so many areas of life that need to be dealt with that figuring out where and how to start can be paralyzingly stressful.

In these moments, we need to identify a thing…one thing… that we can do that will move us in the right direction. And each day, we must continue doing at least one thing that gets us closer to where we want to be. There is no way we can do everything we need to do all at once. Goal pursuit is a marathon, not a sprint. Each day, simply identify one or two things you know need to be done and that you can reasonably do…and then do them. It will require patience, but little by little, you will inevitably see progress. And, eventually, even with only a single daily stroke of a "little axe", the mighty oak will fall.

61

Take Care of Yourself

"If you feel "burnout" setting in, if you feel demoralized and exhausted, it is best, for the sake of everyone, to withdraw and restore yourself." – Dalai Lama

"One of the symptoms of an approaching nervous breakdown is the belief that one's work is terribly important." – Bertrand Russell

"...passengers should be advised to don their own oxygen masks before assisting children with their masks." – Federal Aviation Administration (FAA)

In the busy lives most of us lead, finding time for ourselves can be a significant challenge. We wake up early, get the kids ready for school, work our jobs, feed our kids, get them ready for bed, and then maybe...just maybe...there are a few minutes at the end of the day left for us. Not all of us have kids or work regular hours. However, most of us still struggle to find time to engage in hobbies or personal interests...things that we really enjoy doing.

Because of our lives' nonstop nature, recovery and rejuvenation are essential. We can't do without them. If we try, our stress increases, our patience decreases, our temper shortens, and our days lengthen. And when stress reaches elevated levels and remains there for any length of time, we suffer both physiologically and psychologically.

Today, think of something you love doing. Maybe it's something you haven't done in a long time, but when you did it in the past, you truly enjoyed it. Or, think of something you've always wanted to learn or try. Then, carve out time in your day to do that thing... time that is just for you, nobody else. This might seem like a Herculean task that is simply beyond your capabilities. But it's not.

Wake up a half-hour earlier, and use that time for yourself. Schedule and guard 10-15 minutes once or twice a day for "You Time". You don't have to identify a huge block of time every day. You just need to identify some time most days and then protect that time with all your might.

Life will try to steal those minutes away. It will lure you with phones and computers, kids and spouses. Your mind might, at first, seem in league with Life, doing its best to divert your attention by distracting you with thoughts of chores or sowing guilt about all the things you "need" to do that aren't getting done. Ignore all of it, and protect that time.

To be at our best, we have to take time for ourselves. We have to rejuvenate. We have to recover. So, put your mask on first.

62

You Are Here

"Acceptance doesn't mean resignation; it means understanding that something is what it is and that there's got to be a way through it." –
Michael J. Fox

Here I am…I am here. That doesn't seem like something we should have to remind ourselves of, but it is.

People have different ways of explaining and understanding how they ended up where they currently are, different beliefs about why their lives have ended up the way they have. Some people believe in fate. They believe that they are "supposed" to be where they are and that "everything happens for a reason." Others believe in free will. They believe that they have agency and the ability to direct their lives in whatever way they choose. As a result, these people are where they are because their choices put them there. Still others believe the universe is random. They believe they simply ended up where they did by chance.

Regardless of the reason you believe we are where we are, that's where we are. We might like it, or we might not, but moving forward with any sanity or productivity requires us to accept it.

We must accept our current circumstances instead of trying to convince ourselves we're somewhere we're not (e.g., talk ourselves into believing things that simply aren't true) or continually complaining about and bemoaning the situation without taking any productive action.

Today, pause periodically to assess your current situation. Really take stock of where you are and what's happening. What are you feeling physically and emotionally? What are you thinking about? How do you perceive your situation? Regularly and deliberately forcing ourselves to examine our situation in the present moment allows us to understand our circumstances more thoroughly, creating the conditions for helpful, productive forward movement.

63

Do You

"Be yourself; everyone else is already taken." – Oscar Wilde

"When you are content to be simply yourself and don't compare or compete, everyone will respect you." – Lao Tzu

We compare ourselves to other people all the time. We compare our looks, jobs, positions within our jobs, parenting practices, and many other things. Sometimes we compare ourselves to others hoping we're "better" in some way; however, more frequently we compare ourselves to others, often unconsciously, hoping we're the same as they are. That is, we evaluate the extent to which we differ from others with the hope that we don't fall too far on one side or the other of "the norm".

Regardless of why we compare ourselves to others, the information gained from those comparisons tells us nothing about what's really important…how we compare to ourselves. What matters is whether or not our core values are being lived out through our thoughts and actions. What's important is that our beliefs about how things should be are made abundantly clear by the choices we make throughout the day. Our attention should be focused solely on the extent to which we are doing what we believe we should be doing. The only beneficial comparisons are comparisons we make between ourselves as we were in the past and ourselves as we are in the present.

Throughout the day, notice the frequency with which you compare yourself to other people. What types of comparisons are you making? Do the conclusions you draw from those comparisons influence your thoughts and behaviors in ways that help you live out your values? While you're making the comparisons consider the emotions you're experiencing. Are you experiencing peace and well-being? Or, are you experiencing stress and anxiety?

Make an effort to avoid comparisons between yourself and other people. Instead, focus on your own actions and attitudes, and notice the effect it has on your sense of well-being and contentment. You might be surprised.

64

We Are Simultaneously Sculptures and Sculptors

"Life isn't about finding yourself; it's about creating yourself. So, live the life you imagined." – Henry David Thoreau

When you look at a sculpture, you are looking at the result of a combination of nature (e.g., materials), chance (e.g., scratches and other damage that has occurred since its creation), and choice (e.g., the subject matter and design decided upon by the sculptor). We are the result of the same things.

The physical features we see when we look in the mirror are the result of a combination of our genes (e.g., nature; eye color), things that have happened to us (e.g. chance; scars from accidents), and decisions that we've made (e.g., choice; hair length, physique). Our mental, emotional, and social states are created the same way. There are genetic, dispositional, trait-like factors that affect how we think; emotional experiences of varying types and strengths; and the myriad ways in which we interact with others in the world.

However, chance events…events that were not within our control and did not happen by choice (e.g., personal trauma)… also influence our mental and emotional states and the ways we tend to relate to others.

Finally, our mental, emotional, and social conditions are heavily influenced by our decisions. We choose our priorities, how we perceive situations in our lives, and how we understand and explain what happens to us. By taking control of our thoughts in these ways, we can affect the type and strength of emotions we experience. And both our choice of perceptions and the emotions we feel impact how we talk to and engage with other people.

The bottom line is that although we are certainly the result of genes and chance, we are also the result of intentional choices that we have made and continue to make daily.

Today, consider the type of person you would like to be physically, mentally, emotionally, and spiritually. Then, identify the factors currently influencing your ability to realize that vision, examine those factors in terms of controllability, and make a plan to address those factors that you can control.

Nature and chance certainly affect our circumstances. However, when we think deeply about our situations and realize the depth and breadth of physical, mental, emotional, and spiritual factors within our control, we gain valuable insight into meaningful and immediate adjustments we can make that will bring us closer to realizing our ideal selves.

65

Slow Down

"Unreasonable haste is the direct road to error." – Moliere

"Take time for all things. Great haste makes great waste." – Benjamin Franklin

Most of us live busy lives, and in our fast-paced culture, speed is highly valued. Success is often determined by how many things we complete in a given time or how quickly we finish an assigned task. We do our best to plan the shortest, quickest route when traveling anywhere and do whatever possible to ensure that we get there ahead of our projected arrival time. Although there's nothing inherently wrong with completing tasks or arriving at destinations in as little time as possible, consider the tradeoffs we experience as a result of our obsession with speed.

Do you find yourself regularly stressed out about time? Is your mood negatively affected if you are "running late"? Are you disappointed if it takes you more time than you'd anticipated to finish a task? Do you find your patience challenged when you, your spouse, or your kids aren't moving as quickly as you think they should? Do you feel your stress levels rising in direct proportion to the number of cars blocking your way on the road?

Similarly, have you noticed that as time to complete a task decreases, the number of mistakes increases? Is the quality of work you produce at a comfortable pace different from that of your work at a rushed pace? If not, if the quality of the work is identical in both cases, did you experience any difference in your stress levels and overall well-being? How much time did you actually save by rushing? By speeding through traffic, how many minutes early did you actually arrive? Were those minutes worth the added stress and increased risk you incurred by rushing?

The fact is that when we rush, we increase the likelihood of errors, increase our stress levels, and decrease our levels of patience and well-being, all without improving our overall performance or saving any measurable amounts of time.

Today, notice when you feel rushed or in a hurry. In those moments, take a breath and focus on the process instead of the outcome. Keep your attention on what you are doing rather than the end state you're trying to achieve. In this way, you will keep your focus on your efforts and maintain an ideal energy activation level...both of which will allow you to perform as efficiently and effectively as possible with no rushing or time pressure whatsoever.

66

Embody Your Purpose

"Life is never made unbearable by circumstances, but only by lack of meaning and purpose." – Viktor Frankl

"The soul which has no fixed purpose in life is lost; to be everywhere is to be nowhere." – Montaigne

Because of the busyness of most of our lives it can be very easy to fall into "reaction" mode. We bounce from fire to fire, putting out those we can and simply trying to control those we can't. We find ourselves living through very full days without actually accomplishing anything. And one reason for that is that we have nothing in mind that we're trying to accomplish. We have no purpose.

A purpose provides us with direction and motivation, helps us prioritize our time and activities, and gives a sense of meaning to our lives. You might derive your purpose from a religion, a philosophy, or from an intrinsic feeling you have about why you were put on this Earth. Regardless of what it is or where it comes from, it's important always to keep our purpose in the forefront of our minds.

Today, consider your purpose, and make a deliberate effort to keep that purpose in mind throughout your day, no matter what challenges you face. While thinking about your day, making a to-do list, or creating a schedule for yourself, filter everything through the lens of your purpose. How is each activity related to your purpose? Are you intentionally setting aside time and engaging in activities that align with your purpose?

Hoping that life accidentally creates conditions that allow us to fulfill our unique purposes is unrealistic. Take time today to ensure that your progress toward your purpose does not depend on a favorable roll of the dice.

67

What's My Purpose?

"The two most important days in life are the day you're born and the day you understand why." - Mark Twain

The ultimate purpose of life has been debated for thousands of years. Some have approached the question from the standpoint of a common purpose for all mankind (e.g., Aristotle), and some have suggested that life's purposes are myriad and ephemeral (e.g., Viktor Frankl). However you conceptualize it, though, philosophers and psychologists throughout the ages agree that having a purpose is important for people's overall sense of well-being. But how do you know what your purpose is?

Some people adopt a purpose from the tenets of a religion or a philosophy, while others' purposes stem from more intrinsic sources unique to them. Still others, though, have no idea what their purpose is. If that's you, here are some things you can try that will help you determine your purpose.

Identify some of things you love doing, things you are passionate about and do simply out of enjoyment. These things are done merely because they're fun, not because of any associated outcome or result.

Identify things aligned with your values...things you believe are right, necessary, and important. You might not necessarily love doing them, but you understand their value.

Identify those things that you are good at, especially those things that come naturally or easily to you.

Identify situations when you feel accepted and valued by a group of people. Notice those circumstances when you feel important to people, not for anything you're doing for them, but simply because of who you are as an individual.

Thinking about and identifying the abovementioned things should give you insight into what areas may contain your purpose. You might not find the specific answer right away, but the thought process described will get you a lot closer to identifying your unique purpose.

68

Keep an Open Mind

"Sages learn to unlearn." -Lao Tzu in Tao de Ching

"We can't learn that which we think we already know."- Epictetus

"Even our governing document, the U.S. Constitution, allows for amendments. What if we were quicker to make amendments to our own mental constitutions?" Adam Grant

Keeping an open mind can be one of the toughest but also one of the most important things we can learn to do.

Over the years, each of us amasses beliefs about how we, others, and the world operate. These beliefs then color and influence the way we interpret our surroundings. They lead to assumptions that come quickly and naturally. The problem is that our beliefs are based only on the information we've had access to. Given that we are human and fundamentally limited in myriad ways, we can be certain there is information out there that we've misunderstood or missed altogether. Therefore, it is inevitable that we will have beliefs based on faulty or incomplete information and, as a result, make and act on incorrect assumptions. And this can have a

HUGE influence on the quality of our lives.

There is no surefire way to solve this problem, but endeavoring to develop and maintain an open mind is a great start. Keeping an open mind means staying humble enough to recognize our limitations and acknowledge our ignorance, humble enough to not only admit when we're wrong but to alter our belief system accordingly.

This is not something people like doing for many reasons. As Adam Grant points out in his book, Think Again, "Questioning ourselves makes the world more unpredictable.... Reconsidering something we believe deeply can threaten our identifies, making it feel as if we're losing a part of ourselves." We like feeling certain. We like believing we can predict what will happen, and we often define ourselves in terms of the beliefs we hold. Therefore, changing our beliefs can feel very disorienting and uncomfortable.

But maintaining a willingness to alter our beliefs in the face of new information is critical for our growth, development, and maximal effectiveness. If we can't admit we're wrong, how will we ever understand what is right? If we can't acknowledge we don't know, how will we ever learn? If we never realize that our assumptions stem from faulty beliefs based on incorrect or incomplete information and result in counterproductive or even harmful behavior, how will we ever be able to amend that behavior?

Today, keep an open mind. Question your assumptions. Challenge your beliefs. Admit you don't know or aren't sure about something. Look for new information, and use that information to substantiate or refute your beliefs. Be willing to acknowledge when you're wrong and make the necessary adjustments to your beliefs and behavior based on more accurate and thorough information.

69

Do It For Yourself

"Consider how many do not even know your name and how many will soon forget it, and how those who now praise you will presently blame you." -Marcus Aurelius

"The superior man does not mind failing to get recognition, he is too busy doing the things that entitle him to recognition." - Confucius

All of us are susceptible to the influence of others' opinions. However, what other people think of us is 1) not in our control and 2) volatile, everchanging, and situation-specific. There is inherent uncertainty and doubt built into any endeavor we engage in solely because of how we believe others will think of us. That is, we can never know for sure how people will view us at any given moment or under any given circumstances. Moreover, what some people might find admirable, others find abhorrent. We can't please everybody. We'll never be able to perform to everybody's standards or live up to everybody's expectations. We can, however, live up to our own standards and expectations.

Today, catch yourself when you start wondering what someone else will think. Maybe it's a hairstyle, a choice of clothes, your lunch decision, the speed you drive, or the shows you watch. It could be anything. There is no limit to the type or number of others' opinions we can fixate on. Once you catch yourself wondering what someone else will think about a choice you've made or will make, immediately ask yourself if you are acting in a way that is in line with how you want to be…your standards and expectations of yourself. If the answer is yes, the stress associated with the uncertainty of others' opinions will disappear, and tranquility will ensue.

Trying to please everybody is a Sisyphean task. You can try as hard as you want for as long as you want, but you will never succeed. When you receive praise from one group, you receive condemnation from another. Just please you. Do what you think is the right thing to do. You will have less stress, sleep better, and be able to smile at yourself in the mirror every evening.

70

One Thing At A Time

"To do two things at once is to do neither." -Publilius Syrus

It's fairly predictable that at least once during the day, you will feel stress related to how many responsibilities you are trying to juggle now and in the future. In these moments, we can feel anything ranging from mild stress to something close to overwhelmed panic. There is one simple way to combat this feeling of being swamped and drowning in too many things, and that's to concentrate on only one thing.

As human beings, we can only focus on one thing at a time. That's a fundamental limitation of our attention. When we think we are attending to multiple things, what we are actually doing is shifting attention among those things. That shifting comes with a cost to both the speed and accuracy of whatever we're doing. We function much, much better when, instead, we place all of our focus, attention, and effort on only one thing at a time.

This focus on only one thing reduces stress in two ways. First, we tend to perform better at what we're doing, which minimizes the stress we feel when we don't believe we are competent, capable, or successful. Second, we keep our minds in the present moment, on what is happening now rather than what already happened in the past or what might happen in the future. The present moment is the only place actual control over our circumstances exists. Keeping our attention in the here and now and where we can exercise this control drastically reduces the stress we experience.

Today, notice when you start feeling stressed or overwhelmed by the number of things you need to do. Then stop, identify the most important thing for you to do in that moment, and put all of your effort and attention on that one thing. Once you're finished, repeat that process. In this way, you will make continual progress while minimizing stress and maximizing well-being and productivity.

71

Have To or Get To

"A wise man will make more opportunities than he finds." - Francis Bacon

"Everything can be taken from a man but...the last of the human freedoms— to choose one's attitude in any given set of circumstances."- Viktor Frankl

Each day we have certain responsibilities that must be met. Some of these responsibilities we chose (e.g., taking care of a pet), and some are responsibilities that have been thrust upon us by circumstance (e.g., fixing a broken car). When we think about and discuss these responsibilities, we often think in terms of things we "have" to do. An equally valid...and more productive...way of thinking about the situation, though, is rather than "having" to do something, you "get" to do something.

When we frame life's circumstances as opportunities rather than obligations, we tend to be more open to growth and development, experience less stress and frustration, and maintain much better attitudes. And this is a choice we get to make in each and every life situation we encounter.

Today, notice when you are thinking in terms of things you "have" to do. Notice your attitude, mindset, stress levels, and physiology (e.g., muscle tension, breathing). Then, shift your perspective to one of "getting" to do those things, of having the opportunity to do those things. Notice how that shift boosts your mood, relaxes your body, decreases stress, and increases gratitude. When we think in terms of "get to", we are grateful for the chance to take care of whatever needs to be taken care of.

If you have kids, this is a great way to teach them to address their own responsibilities with much better attitudes. When you ask your child to do something and hear, "Do I have to?", simply respond by saying, "No. You get to." Then, follow that statement up with some guidance that helps your child reframe the situation. This will help them to reframe challenging situations they face on their own more easily as they get older.

72

Noticing Opportunities

"To hell with circumstances; I create opportunities." - Bruce Lee

"Our lives are defined by opportunities, even the ones we miss." -F. Scott Fitzgerald

Opportunities don't just show up. They manifest themselves as a result of our attention, confidence, and motivation.

If we want to maximize the number of opportunities in our lives, we first must ensure that we're paying attention to the right things. As human beings, the only things that make it into our awareness and, therefore, become part of our reality are things we pay attention to. Every day we are constantly bombarded by stimuli vying for our attention; however, human attention is a finite resource. We can't pay attention to everything. So, we have to make sure our attention is focused on the area in which we would like opportunities to emerge.

Second, we must believe in ourselves. If we have confidence in our abilities, we will see opportunities in situations that less confident people won't. We will recognize possibilities for growth and development in situations that others dismiss or don't even notice.

Third, we must stay motivated. Strong and consistent motivation, even in the face of setbacks, is required to ensure we find ourselves in situations that can be turned into opportunities by our unswerving attention and impenetrable confidence.

Opportunities are there. We just have to recognize them, believe in our abilities, and maintain our motivation. Today, look around for your opportunities. Choose to view every situation you're in as an opportunity for something…some kind of growth, some kind of improvement, some kind of learning…something. Opportunities don't simply poof into existence. They emerge from our perceptions.

73

Confidence – Personal Experience

"Do not let what you cannot do interfere with what you can do."
-John Wooden

"If you hear a voice inside you that says, 'You cannot paint,' then by all means paint, and that voice will be silenced." -Vincent Van Gogh

According to eminent psychologist Albert Bandura, confidence…or self-efficacy…is affected by four things: past experience, vicarious experience (watching others), persuasion, and our physical state. Because confidence is a crucial factor in not only how well we perform but in our overall sense of well-being, we will discuss each of these sources of confidence, taking them one day at a time.

Confidence depends heavily on our past experiences. However, it is not the experiences themselves, but our interpretations of those experiences that determine our confidence levels. Many people believe that for confidence to improve, we must experience success, but this is not the case. Success and failure both have the potential to increase or decrease confidence depending on why we think that success/failure happened.

Confidence is positively affected by success when we 1) know what we did to be successful and 2) believe that what we did to be successful is in our control...that we can repeat those things at will. If, however, we attribute success to things outside of our control (e.g., luck) or have no idea what we did that led to success, then our confidence is not likely to increase.

Failure affects confidence in the same way but with an added belief that's important. Confidence is positively affected by failure when:
1. We know what we did that led to failure.
2. Believe that those factors that led to failure are within our control.
3. Believe that we are capable of doing those things correctly the next time around.

Failure only negatively impacts our confidence if we don't know why we failed or don't believe that we can do anything about the factors that led to failure...either because those factors are out of our control or we don't have the necessary skills or abilities to change them.

Today, tune into your own confidence associated with the various activities you engage in throughout the day. Regardless of whether you succeeded or failed the last time you did that task, ask yourself why you succeeded/failed, identify the factors that led to success/failure, and repeat the steps you took to succeed and adjust the steps you took when you failed. If you've never done a particular task before and, therefore, can't draw upon direct experience, think about a similar situation in which you succeeded or failed and engage in the same process described above.

Whether you succeeded or failed in the past, using experience to boost your confidence can be extremely effective, but only if you think about that experience in terms of lessons learned about things you can control.

74

Confidence – Watching Others

"Everyone you will ever meet knows something you don't." -Bill Nye

The second source of confidence is vicarious experience. This is when our confidence is influenced by watching others do something. Just like personal experience, the success or failure of the individual we are watching isn't what affects our confidence. What affects our confidence are our beliefs about:

1.　Why the person succeeded/failed.

2.　Whether the factors that led to success/failure are within our control.

3.　Our ability to repeat factors that led to success or correct factors that led to failure.

Today, take the time to watch other people do things that maybe you're not confident doing. You might find these people in your own environment (e.g., people you work with), or you may need to search elsewhere (e.g., online videos). Wherever you find them, watch people doing what you're worried about doing. Pay particular attention not to whether they succeed or fail, but to what they do that leads to success or failure. What specific steps are they taking? What strategies and behaviors are they choosing? Also, pay attention to their body language. Based on that body language, what attitude or mindset do you believe that person adopted? If you have the opportunity to question the person, ask about what they did mentally to prepare for what they were doing and what mental strategies or techniques they used to stay focused, positive, energized, and engaged.

Again, like personal experience, vicarious experience can boost our confidence, whether we're watching someone succeed or fail. What matters is that we identify what they did that led to success/ failure, pinpoint which of those factors are controllable, and take the necessary steps to repeat what worked (i.e., success) and avoid what didn't (i.e., failure).

75

Confidence – Persuasion

"I have a confidence in my life that comes from standing tall on my own two feet."- Jane Fonda

"We must have perseverance and above all confidence in ourselves. We must believe that we are gifted for something and that this thing must be attained." -Marie Curie

The third source of confidence is persuasion. Persuasion can come from other people or from ourselves. If coming from other people, persuasion most effectively boosts confidence when it comes from people we know and trust, people we look up to and whose opinions matter to us. However, persuasion doesn't have to come from without; it can also come from within. We can persuade ourselves through our self-talk, deliberately chosen thoughts designed to enhance our confidence.

Persuasion can boost our confidence by changing what we're focused on, how we perceive our situation, or how we perceive our own abilities. Whether persuasion emanates from others or ourselves, it directs our attention to the aspects of our circumstances and qualities of ourselves most relevant to our confidence. This ensures that we perceive our situation in as productive a way as possible. The most effective persuasion turns our attention toward those things we can control (e.g. attitude, effort, strategies, behaviors) and convinces us that we are capable of leveraging these things in a way that will lead to success.

Today, use persuasion to affect confidence in both yourself and others. If you're not confident about something, tune into your self-talk and intentionally choose thoughts that keep you focused on things you can control. If you notice someone else whose confidence is shaky, persuade that person. Help that person recognize controllable factors within their situation and remember the skills and abilities they can leverage to be successful.

76

Confidence – Physical State

"A little bit of stage fright, then I'm ready." Faith Hill

The final source of confidence is our beliefs about our physical state. When we are in situations that matter to us, situations in which how well we do is important to us, our sympathetic nervous system (i.e. fight/flight/freeze) kicks in. This initiates specific physiological changes, including increases in heart rate and muscle tension, rapid breathing, perspiration, and nausea. Although these physical changes are normal, natural, and predictable, how we perceive these physical changes can vary.

If we interpret these physical effects as indicators that we are not ready to go, our confidence levels will lower. Whereas, if we interpret these physical effects as indicators that we are ready, our confidence levels will rise. When we understand and interpret these naturally occurring physical changes as simply our bodies preparing us for action, recognizing that we are feeling exactly the way we should be before an important event boosts our confidence.

The next time you find yourself in a situation where the quality of your performance matters, notice what is going on with your body. Recognize the shift in breathing, muscle tension, and breathing. Then, remind yourself that your body is doing precisely what it is designed to do. It's preparing itself for action, naturally setting the conditions for you to be at your best.

77

Check Your Assumptions

"Begin challenging your own assumptions. Your assumptions are your windows on the world. Scrub them off every once in a while, or the light won't come in." Alan Alda

"If we worked on the assumption that what is true really is true, then there would be little hope for advance." Orville Wright

"Assumptions are made, and most assumptions are wrong." Albert Einstein

The assumptions we make drive the actions we take.

Our brains are wired to prioritize information they think is most relevant at any given time. Because there is so much information out there, though, our brains have developed systematic shortcuts that provide us with the most relevant information in the shortest amount of time. This means we don't automatically take the time to become aware of all available information before drawing conclusions about reality. In fact, the opposite occurs. Our brains take in only the amount of information they think they need to produce a useful interpretation of our environments, an interpretation that will allow us to take productive action. These are assumptions.

Assumptions are the conclusions we draw from the limited information we're aware of at any given moment. Most of the time, we move passively through the world while our brains unconsciously determine where our attention should go and what the information coming in means. Over time, we develop habitual ways of interpreting our environments that cause our thoughts to occur automatically and outside our awareness. This can cause problems.

Today, tune into your assumptions. Notice when your judgments about people and interpretations of situations occur immediately. Recognize when the conclusions you draw are based on a minimal amount of information that you have not taken the time to consider thoroughly. Then, pause and gather more information. Check your assumptions for accuracy. You might be right…but you might not.

78

Benefits of the Benefit of the Doubt

"You have no idea what [people's] reality is, you have no idea what they've been through—and how much more empathetic and patient might you be if you did. Or better, if you gave them every benefit of the doubt." -Ryan Holiday

When interacting with others, we can quickly jump to conclusions about their thoughts, intentions, and actions. We can even go so far as to not only assume we know what they're thinking and why they're doing what they are right now, but assume that we know the underlying values and beliefs that make that person who they are at their core. Jumping to conclusions in this way can not only result in us making bad decisions based on faulty information but can result in strained and broken relationships with people we really care about.

Today, give people the benefit of the doubt. When you see them acting in a way you think is questionable or even objectionable, assume that they are acting in good faith, that they have good intentions. Remember that there are many possible intentions driving any one action. For example, if I see a child throwing a rock at my window, they might be trying to get my attention (as my daughter, unfortunately, did the other day), or they might be trying to damage my house. The action is the same, but the intention is very different. So, instead of jumping to the conclusion that someone is acting out of malice, spite, or indifference, give that person the benefit of the doubt. Assume that the person is doing their best to act in a just, virtuous way. If that act is, in your opinion, very obviously counterproductive, assume that the person simply doesn't have the information you have because if they did, they would make a different choice.

Giving people the benefit of the doubt in this way will all but eliminate anger. It will help you avoid unnecessary arguments, misunderstandings, and confrontations. Compassion replaces anger. This compassion will result in very different actions on your part. It may end up fostering a new relationship, strengthening a tenuous relationship, or sustaining a valued relationship. What you will definitely notice, though, is an immediate reduction in stress and negative emotions…and that, in and of itself, is worth its weight in gold.

79

Recognizing the Fundamental Attribution Error

From PEANUTS by Charles Schultz

LINUS: Why are you always so anxious to criticize me?
LUCY: I just think I have a knack for seeing other people's faults.
LINUS: What about your own faults?
LUCY: I have a knack for overlooking them.

Ever notice that when someone does something you don't like, you assume the behavior is a good indicator of that person's personality and values? Ever notice, too, how quickly you justify your own bad behavior in terms of some temporary or situational factor influencing you in that moment? This tendency to attribute others' bad behaviors to internal traits and our own bad behaviors to situational circumstances is known as the fundamental attribution error.

Succumbing to this error happens frequently. For example, if someone is driving slowly in the left lane, you might attribute this behavior to that person being a disrespectful idiot. Whereas, if you find yourself driving slowly in the left lane one day, you might attribute this behavior to being distracted by a child, a phone call, or deep and important thoughts. In other words, the same behavior is attributed to one cause (momentary distraction) when we do it and another cause (being an idiot) when someone else does it.

The fundamental attribution error shows up in our lives every day and can significantly affect our relationships with other people. Today, notice your tendency to judge somebody else as inherently flawed because of some behavior you witnessed. Notice, too, the speed with which you explain away your own mistakes as anomalies and not at all indicative of who you truly are as a person. Then, question your assumptions...from both sides. What situational circumstances might have led to the behavior you witnessed in the other person? What deeply held, underlying value or belief might have influenced your own behavior?

80

Goals, Process, and Happiness

"The future is completely open, and we are writing it moment to moment." -Pema Chödrön

Setting and pursuing goals is a great way to help you avoid stagnation, continue to grow and develop, and stay focused on things that matter to you. However, fixating solely and exclusively on the goals themselves...the outcomes we desire... can be counterproductive.

When our only focus is on the goal itself and our desire to achieve it, we are, by definition, living in a state of dissatisfaction with the present. We are unhappy with how things currently are and believe that things will improve once we ultimately obtain this objective we've identified for ourselves. This is a problem for two reasons. First, we often ignore and fail to put effort toward engaging in the small, individual actions necessary for goal achievement and, therefore, lessen the likelihood that we'll achieve our goal. Second, and at least as importantly, we fail to recognize and appreciate the good that we have right in front of us, all of the things in our lives we should be grateful for, and that could contribute to our happiness right now, in this moment, if we simply noticed them.

Today, continue your goal pursuit...always keeping in mind the reason why you want to achieve your goal, but avoid fixating on the goal itself. Instead, identify a few realistic actions and attitudes you can put into practice during the day that will move you closer to your goal achievement. Also, take time to reflect on the aspects of your life, right now as it currently is, that you are grateful for. Remind yourself that happiness does not depend on future outcomes (goal achievement). You can be happy in this moment by fully appreciating and attending to the many gifts in your life as it is in the here and now.

81

Value Intentions Over Actions

"Who we are is about not what we do, but why we tell ourselves we do it." –Jodi Picoult

From the outside, behavior looks the same regardless of why we do it. But why we do something is at least, if not more, important than what we do.

Imagine you see a person helping an older person across a street. You might praise that person, mentally or out loud, as a wonderful, virtuous person…and maybe they are. Imagine, however, other possible motives that person might have for helping the senior across the street that aren't so altruistic. Maybe the "helping" individual is using the behavior as a distraction in order to steal something. Or, maybe the helper is the person's employee who is trying to curry favor with the boss. The point is that the behavior is the same in each case, but the motivations and intentions behind the behavior are very different.

Think, too, about some of your own actions. If you've donated clothes, is the reason primarily because you wanted to do something to help those less fortunate or because you wanted a free and easy place to discard your old clothes that will provide you with a tax write-off? If you've helped someone pick up something they dropped in front of you, did you do it because you believed it was just the right thing to do or because you worried about what others around you would think about you if you simply stood by and watched the person struggle while doing nothing?

Today, recognize your tendency to judge people by their behaviors and, instead, judge them by their intentions. If you don't know their intentions, ask. If asking isn't possible, assume the best intentions. Absent confirmed contradictory information, giving people the benefit of the doubt is a great thing to do. However, don't just limit your awareness to how you judge others' behaviors. Pay particular attention to your own motives as well. Why are you doing what you're doing? What are you ultimately trying to accomplish? Are your intentions aligned with the values you hold and think are important?

82

Helping Without Helping

"If a man knows where to get good advice, it is as though he could supply it himself." -Goethe

Often friends will tell us about problems they are dealing with in their lives. They may bring up these issues organically during a normal conversation or seek you out deliberately to talk about something bothering them. Sometimes they want you to provide answers or advice, while other times, they simply want a sounding board they can trust.

When you find yourself in these situations, unless you have a working crystal ball, the best thing to do is ask the person what they want from you. Ask them if they are looking for advice or just want to vent. Let them know that you are fine with either, are there for them, and will support them however you can. Regardless of whether you offer advice or not, there are two components that the conversation should have: clarifying the problem and generating solutions. If you plan to offer answers or advice, whatever you bring in the way of guidance should come once the other two components have been completed.

The next time a friend comes to you with a problem, make sure they're clear on what the problem actually is. This may involve them defining terms like "hard" or "distant" or "jackass". It also may involve asking questions about why they see the situation as a problem, what the "bad" part is and what "good" would look like.

Once both of you understand the problem, ask about what has already been done to address the problem and what else might be done that they haven't thought of yet. The goal here is to allow the individual with the problem to generate realistic solutions they believe could be effective. In this way, they feel empowered by their ability to address the issue plaguing them successfully. They have a viable solution they are likely to implement because they are the one who came up with it.

If, after clarifying the problem and prompting them to generate solutions, they've come up with nothing, that is when you might offer some of your own sage wisdom. This process is tricky and should be executed with complete care and empathy for that individual and their situation. However, you are a person they care about and trust. That's why they came to you. So, any useful, practical information you can provide is likely to be welcome after the failed brainstorming session.

83

Be How You Want To Be

"Any man could, if he were inclined, be the sculptor of his own brain." Santiago Ramon y Cajal –Winner, 1906 Nobel Prize in Physiology or Medicine

Given all of the discussion about personality that pervades both our pop culture and workplace environments, it can be easy to succumb to the belief that you are defined by characteristics "hardwired" into your very being. From this perspective, you were born with unique strengths and weaknesses, tendencies and proclivities, and qualities and features you must recognize and fully embrace in order to navigate and interact with the world as effectively as possible. This perspective is not wrong…but it's dangerously misleading.

It's true that we were born, and continue to be, unique. It's also true that we have numerous strengths, weaknesses, and other individual characteristics that tend to be fairly stable over time. However, it is NOT true that these aspects of ourselves are fixed or that we are destined to be exactly how we are now for the rest of time. The truth is that our brains are malleable and are, in fact, changing right now as a result of reading these words.

Each time we think, do, or feel something, a specific pattern of neurons fire together. When this happens regularly, our brains figure out how to make the connections among those neurons stronger and more efficient. This is called neuroplasticity and is why your thoughts, attitudes, emotions, and behaviors are not fated to remain the same for eternity.

Today, notice when you fall into the trap of believing that some aspect of yourself is hardwired and, therefore, unchangeable. It might be your tendency to view things optimistically vs. pessimistically; your level of introversion vs. extroversion; or your math, reading, art, or physical skills. Whatever it is, notice your belief that this aspect of you is "just part of who you are". Again, this belief isn't wrong...the characteristic IS part of who you are...right now. However, because it's part of you right now doesn't mean it has to stay part of you forever. So, if after noticing these characteristics there are some that you would like to be different, make them different. Begin rewiring your brain by making deliberate efforts to think and act differently. Changes won't happen overnight, but with consistent and intentional effort over time, they WILL happen.

84

Choose Courage

"I learned that courage was not the absence of fear, but the triumph over it. The brave man is not he who does not feel afraid, but he who conquers that fear." -Nelson Mandela

We tend to spend much of our lives avoiding things we're afraid of. There's nothing wrong with trying to minimize the number of difficulties we encounter in life; however, regardless of how diligently we try to eliminate them, challenges and difficulties that threaten our well-being will inevitably arise. When this happens, how we perceive those challenges will make a big difference in the emotions we experience and the behaviors we choose.

Today, when challenges arise, especially ones that cause fear, doubt, uncertainty, and stress, choose to see them as opportunities to practice the virtue of courage. Courage does not develop in times of peace and tranquility, times when everything in life is going according to plan. We only cultivate courage when we experience situations that require us to be courageous, situations when we are scared, nervous, and outside our comfort zones.

So, as you move through your day, notice when you are experiencing fear, doubt, and discomfort associated with a challenging situation you face. Then, embrace those challenges and face your fear. View that situation as an opportunity and be grateful for the chance to practice courage.

85

Self-Talk - Choose and Use Thoughts

"The happiness of your life depends on the quality of your thoughts."
-Marcus Aurelius

Deliberately chosen thoughts can be very powerful, a fact known for thousands of years. Whether the thoughts go by the name of mantra, power statement, or self-talk, these intentionally chosen thoughts are helpful for three reasons:

1. The thoughts direct our attention to where our attention should be. By choosing our thoughts, we can ensure that our attention lands on the most beneficial things rather than simply hoping we will pay attention when, where, and how we need to.

2. Because humans can only focus on one thing at a time, keeping our attention on these purposely chosen thoughts helps prevent other thoughts or things in our environments from distracting us.

3. Because distraction is something that can only be mitigated and not eliminated, these purposeful thoughts can help us regain our focus when inevitable distractions occur. These

purposefully chosen thoughts serve as a sort of life preserver we can grasp as soon as we become aware we are drowning in an ocean of distraction.

What's a situation you will likely face that might benefit from you having a deliberately chosen thought in mind? Is there a time or circumstance in which you could use a confidence boost? Is there an activity during which you tend to be hampered frequently by distraction? Is there a situation during which you know that you are at your best when you are feeling a certain way or focusing on a certain thing?

Today, choose a thought you can benefit from and put it into practice. It might take some time before you identify the best thought for you and develop the habit of using that thought in beneficial ways. However, with practice and dedication, you will experience the attentional, emotional, and behavioral advantages of deliberately chosen self-talk.

86

Remember the Log in Your Own Eye

"Why do you see the speck that is in your brother's eye, but do not notice the log that is in your own eye?"
Matthew 7:3, Bible – English Standard Version

Noticing other people's flaws is easy; recognizing our own is much harder. Part of the reason for that is something known as the fundamental attribution bias. This is our tendency to explain others' behaviors in terms of stable personality characteristics while explaining our own behavior in terms of temporary situational factors. For example, we might see a parent snap at a child for no apparent reason and label that parent as a "jackass", a "hothead", or a "bad parent". Whereas, if we realize that we have snapped at our own child, we might explain that behavior as the result of fatigue, hunger, or being at the end of a very stressful day.

Today, tune in to those moments when you notice something wrong with somebody else or something you think somebody did that they shouldn't have. Instead of jumping to conclusions and judging their character based on your limited knowledge about the situation, turn your attention inward. Remember times when you have behaved in the same or a similar manner. Why did you do it? Was it because of something inherently wrong with you, or was there some other factor(s) that affected your behavior in those moments?

Getting into the habit of suspending judgment by remembering our own snafus can very quickly reduce anger and increase both empathy and compassion. In fact, instead of condemning that individual, you might find yourself wanting to help.

87

Use the Antidote

"You mainly feel the way you think." -Albert Ellis

Negative emotions such as anger, fear, and jealousy can quickly erode our well-being and poison our relationships with others. What's important to remember, though, is that these emotions are simply the result of our thoughts. What we choose to think about our situations, how we explain the things happening around us, is what will determine the emotions we experience. So, the antidotes to these poisonous emotions are healthier thoughts.

Today, notice when you experience nervousness, fear, anger, or envy. Then, ask yourself why you're feeling that way. The answer should come to you in the form of an explanation following the word "because". Maybe it's, "Because he said my project sucked," or "Because the last time I tried talking to her about something this important she stopped talking to me." Whatever follows the "because" is your perception, the way you are currently thinking about the situation. However, every situation has myriad ways that it can be perceived. So, choose a different way. Choose a way to think about your situation that evokes more positive and productive emotions, emotions that allow you to be at your best and experience peace, tranquility, and equanimity.

Force yourself to become aware of what emotion you're feeling and why you're feeling it. Then, practice shifting your perspective, altering how you see that situation. That deliberate shift to more effective thinking is the antidote for poisonous emotions.

88

The Importance of Feeling Words

"I suppose it's tempting, if the only tool you have is a hammer, to treat everything as if it were a nail." -Abraham Maslow

In her book Atlas of the Heart, renowned emotions researcher Brené Brown argued that developing a detailed, nuanced, and thorough emotional vocabulary is critical. There are myriad emotions we experience, and many of those emotions feel similar to, but not exactly the same as, others. More importantly, although some emotions feel similar (e.g., envy, jealousy), they are not experienced for the same reasons…and those reasons matter. This is important to keep in mind for our kids, spouses, and friends… as well as ourselves. That is, the accuracy of our assessment of our own emotions and the information we receive from those we love about their emotions will depend largely on the number of emotion words available to describe those emotions.

Today, tune into how you are feeling and then label that emotion. If you find yourself gravitating toward broad, general descriptions (e.g., angry), challenge yourself to find a more specific name for the emotion you are feeling (e.g., frustrated). If you have kids, encourage them to do the same thing. For example, if your daughter tells you she's "nervous" about the oral report she's giving the next day, offer some other words that might more specifically describe how she's feeling (e.g., concerned, worried, scared, petrified).

Cognitive psychologist Albert Ellis pointed out, "Feelings largely cause behavior. The way you feel, and how strongly, will greatly influence how you behave in a situation." So, the better our emotional vocabulary, the better our understanding of our everyday experiences. And the better our understanding of our experiences, the better able we are to take proactive, beneficial action in our lives and the lives of those we love.

89

Want What You Have

"It is in no man's power to have whatever he wants; but he has it in his power not to wish for what he hasn't got, and cheerfully make the most of the things that do come his way." –Seneca

"Do not spoil what you have by desiring what you have not; remember that what you now have was once among the things you only hoped for."- Epicurus

We spend an inordinate amount of life focused on what we don't have. We wish for material things, for different circumstances, for people to act better than they do, and for ourselves to be better than we are. We quickly and easily identify aspects of our lives that aren't ideal and spend a great deal of time and effort trying to change those things. Why? Because we're not happy with how things are right now.

But what if we were?

What if we were content with things just as they are in this moment? What if, instead of wanting what we don't have, we wanted what we do have? What if, instead of imagining how wonderful life would be when some aspect of it changed, we recognized how wonderful life is the way things currently are?

Today, instead of fixating on things you believe to be missing from your life, focus on what you already have and why those things are good. Think about all of the things you have now that, at one point in time, you didn't have...and feel grateful. Think about the number of life circumstances and things you own that, not that long ago, were nothing more than desires, hopes, and dreams. Spend today wanting you have.

90

Let Go of the List

"Only one link of the chain of destiny can be handled at a time."
-Winston Churchill

The best way to get things done is to stop thinking about all the things you want to do. Instead, wake up, choose one thing to do, put your entire focus on that one thing, put all your effort into completing that one thing, and then repeat that process until you go to sleep.

It's certainly useful to take stock of your day, week, month... life. We have to do that from time to time to get a grasp on what responsibilities we have, how we will prioritize those responsibilities, and how we plan to meet those responsibilities given the constraints placed on us by ourselves, others, and our environments. However, once we know what needs to be done, which responsibilities must be prioritized and met today, we need to let go of the list of outcomes and just focus, one at a time, on the smaller tasks we need to do to achieve those larger objectives.

Today, when you realize your attention has shifted from the present moment to your long list of responsibilities, ask yourself what one thing you could do in that moment that would be maximally productive. Then, immerse yourself in the completion of that activity. Once you've completed the activity, start over. Ask yourself again what the most important thing you could be doing is, and then completely immerse yourself in that activity until it's finished. In this way, we ensure that our efforts are as efficient and effective as possible, we reduce the inefficiency associated with shifting our attention and effort back and forth between different activities, and we minimize the likelihood of becoming stressed out and overwhelmed by the sheer volume of things we need to do.

91

What Should I Do?

"We must make the choices that allow us to fulfill the deepest capacities of our real selves." -Thomas Merton

Decisions are an unavoidable part of life. We make hundreds of them a day. Sometimes, the decisions we make are straightforward and come naturally; other times, they're more complex and require reflection. The interesting thing about that, though, is that it's not necessarily the most important or impactful decisions that are the hardest to make.

Why might that be?

When making decisions, there are two things we should consider to help us maximize the likelihood that the decisions we make will be ones we won't regret down the road. First, prioritize decisions. Some decisions are important, and some aren't. Some decisions need to be made now, and some don't. Second, while considering the different things we're deciding between/among, make the deciding factor the extent to which each possibility aligns with your values, beliefs, and overall purpose.

How do those two considerations impact the ease with which we make decisions and our long-term comfortability with our choices?

When we tackle decisions in order of priority, we focus on only one decision at a time. When our attention is fully engaged on the most important decision, clarity follows.

Also, the most certain way to tranquility and peace is to ensure that our actions match our values, that we actually behave in ways we believe we should behave. Therefore, deliberately choosing options aligned with our values is the surest way to avoid second-guessing and "buyer's remorse".

The next time you encounter a decision, ask yourself a few questions. Is it an important decision? If so, is it a decision that needs to be made right now? If it is, which of the options available to you do you believe best represents your values and beliefs? Which option do you believe will move you further down the road toward the fulfillment of your purpose?

92

Decide to Win

"May your choices reflect your hopes, not your fears." -Nelson Mandela

Every day we make decisions, and whether we're talking about taking or refraining from action, the choice often comes down to risk vs. safety. This choice takes many forms, but the way I like to conceptualize it is, "Are you trying to win, or are you trying not to lose?"

We can easily become the slaves of our fears. When this happens, each decision we make pushes us closer to the known, to the comfort of the familiar, and away from the possibility of failure. Taking risks and accepting the possibility of failure can be very difficult for many people, especially when the perceived consequences of that failure are very high. However, sometimes we get so enamored with and engrossed in comfort that we forget how we got comfortable in the first place. We forget the discomfort we had to experience in the past to get to the comfort we are experiencing in the present.

Today, when faced with a choice, one that really matters, check in with your emotions. What are you feeling? Are your emotions impacting your decision-making? When making the decision, what rationales are you telling yourself for why one option would be better than another? And, once you do make a choice, ask yourself the hard question…Did that choice get you closer to winning, or simply keep you from losing?

93

Who Is Your Ruler?

"There is a need for someone against which our characters can measure themselves. Without a ruler, you won't make the crooked straight."
-Seneca

L iving a life of flourishing and fulfillment requires us to think and act in accordance with our values. So, we must first identify our core values and beliefs before we can thrive. Once we are fully aware of our values and beliefs, we then need to align our thinking and behavior with those values and beliefs. And the best way to start doing that is to watch someone else model the mindsets, attitudes, and behaviors we would like to emulate.

Without a clear picture of "right", we can't ever really know whether our attitudes and behaviors are truly aligned with our values. So, once we've chosen the values that will be the guiding forces in our lives, we need to identify somebody who embodies those values and emulate how that person lives. Ideally, this person will be someone with whom we regularly engage and who is willing to serve as a mentor. However, we can learn from people we admire even without direct contact. For example, we will never meet Benjamin Franklin in person. But, if we believe that Benjamin Franklin embodied the values that truly matter to us, we can read his works and follow his suggestions about how to behave (e.g., journaling about values).

Today, think about one or two people you believe embody the characteristics and values you would like to live by. If they are alive, reach out and see if you can begin a dialogue with them. If not, make time to regularly read what they've written and what's been written about them. In either case, choose one or two behaviors and attitudes you admire in these people and immediately put those into practice in meaningful, tangible ways. At first, this might seem awkward and possibly inauthentic. However, with time comes a sense of naturalness, authenticity, and the regularly experienced peace, confidence, and tranquility that accompany a flourishing and thriving life.

94

What is "Good"?

"I have often wondered how it is that every man loves himself more than all the rest of men, but yet sets less value on his own opinion of himself than on the opinion of others." -Marcus Aurelius

Every day we reflect on the outcomes of our behaviors. We evaluate how our actions and interactions turn out. The goal of these reflections is to understand whether we were effective or not. So, an important question to consider is, "How do we decide if we've done well?"

One way we might answer this question is in terms of what other people think. What are other people thinking about us? Do others believe we did well? What are others saying about us? How are others reacting to what we did? Based on the answers to these questions, we might draw a conclusion about the extent to which we were effective.

Another way to answer the question is terms of what we think. Do we believe that our actions were effective? Do we believe that our actions were in line with our intentions? Were our intentions in line with our values? Did we meet the standard we had in mind or do better than we've done in the past? Answers to these questions also allow us to draw conclusions about our effectiveness.

Other people's judgments are precarious things on which to base our beliefs about our effectiveness, because other people may not define "good" in the same way we do. Moreover, we have no control over other people's moods or how much attention they pay to us. A much more consistent and predictable way to evaluate our effectiveness is to assess the extent to which we met objectives that were set or improved from one iteration to the next.

Today, be aware of the measuring tool you're using to determine your effectiveness. If you realize that you're relying heavily on others' judgments, shift your focus to your own judgments and prioritize evaluative tools that are objective and stable in nature.

95

Gratitude: If a Little's Good, More's Better

"Cultivate the habit of being grateful for every good thing that comes to you, and to give thanks continuously. And because all things have contributed to your advancement, you should include all things in your gratitude." –Ralph Waldo Emerson

Years of research have shown that gratitude is associated with positive emotions, strong relationships, and life satisfaction. For some of us, though, perceiving life through the lens of gratitude does not come naturally. So, if you sometimes have trouble cultivating gratitude, here are some suggestions.

First, set aside time devoted to experiencing gratitude. This can be at any time of the day you choose and doesn't have to be for long. But designating times to cultivate gratitude deliberately will make you more likely to overcome life's inertia.

Another thing you can do is become more sensitive to times when you feel dissatisfied with your life. Awareness of dissatisfaction can serve as a mental cue, a red flag, that you need to change your perspective. In these moments, shift your thinking from whatever is causing your dissatisfaction to something you have in your life that you value and are grateful for. It might be your health, a child, an upcoming vacation…anything you can focus on that allows you to be grateful.

Also, rather than switching your focus from something you're dissatisfied with to something you're grateful for, another arguably more effective approach is to change the way you perceive the thing with which you are dissatisfied. That is, instead of distracting yourself from the current situation you're unhappy about, choose to perceive your circumstances in a way that allows you to be grateful, whatever those circumstances might be.

Regularly and deliberately choosing to experience gratitude can quickly and drastically affect our stress levels, relationships, and overall well-being.

96

Praise Is Nice, But...

"For when you have done good, what more, oh man, do you wish? Is it not enough that what you did was in agreement with your nature and do you seek a recompense for this? As if the eye asked a return for seeing or the feet for walking..." –Marcus Aurelius

There is no doubt that praise is nice to get; however, as with any reward we receive, it's easy to start behaving in specific ways solely to get that reward. That is, it can be easy for the reasons why we engage in a certain behavior to move from "because it's the right thing to do" to "because people will notice and praise me for it."

The problem with this shift in our behavioral rationale is twofold. First, we will never behave in a grounded, predictable way that is consistently aligned with our values because we will only choose behaviors we believe will be viewed positively by others. Second, we can't control others' perceptions, so we can never really be sure what other people will find praiseworthy.

The much better choice is to choose behaviors based on the extent to which you believe those behaviors are correct. In other words, do the right thing because it's the right thing to do…not because of any praise or additional reward you might receive.

97

What DON'T You Know?

O ur society values quick and decisive action over hesitant and cautious deliberation. We admire the person who asserts themselves by confidently donning the leadership mantle and authoritatively issuing guidance and direction amid chaos. There are certainly times when this is an important and effective way to handle circumstances. However, most of our lives rarely play out in ways that make the need for split-second choices about important decisions necessary.

Instead, the more effective approach to handling life's challenges is usually the opposite approach. Rather than reacting in the moment to the limited information we currently have, we should pause, gather as much information as we can, consider all information carefully, and then act. Life is complex, with many different factors affecting us at any given moment. So, taking the time to gather and thoroughly analyze information helps us understand our situations as well as possible and maximize the likelihood that our decisions will not be ones we ultimately regret.

Today, notice the times when you feel compelled to act quickly. In these moments, pause and ask yourself if it's truly necessary that a decision is made right now. Take stock of the quality and quantity of information you currently have and ask yourself if there is information missing that might make your decision easier. By taking a little bit of extra time on the front end of decisions, we can save ourselves a great deal of time, stress, and possibly guilt on the back end.

98

Basing the Future on the Past

*"The assumption that things that have been conjured in the past
will always be conjured is the principle not of rational but of animal
behavior."* C. S. Lewis

The past is a terrific predictor of the future...except when
it isn't.

Our expectations of the future tend to be based primarily on
the past. For example, if you try a new route from home to work
and it takes you 15 minutes, you expect that same route to take
15 minutes the next day. If you serve your child salmon for dinner
and she likes it, you expect your child to like salmon the next time
you serve it. The past is how we decide what to do in the future
because how things went in the past is usually a great indicator of
how things will go in the future. Usually...but not always.

Imagine that for three days your new route from home to work
consistently took 15 minutes, but then the next day it took 25
minutes, and the day after that it took 30 minutes. There are many
reasons why this might happen:

1. A school along the route was out and is now back in session.
2. Construction just resumed somewhere on the road and is backing up traffic.
3. Random accidents occurred along the route.

Similarly, if you're a parent, chances are you've experienced the disappointing and disorienting revulsion your child showed to the food they gladly ate previously with no issues whatsoever. In all of these cases, the past did not serve as an accurate predictor of the future.

Today, be aware of your expectations and assumptions based on the past. Rather than rely solely on the past to predict how the future might go, gather more information. Instead of assuming that something happening a certain way last time means it will happen the same way this time, take a fresh look at the available information. This doesn't mean that we can't use the past as one source of information; it just means that we shouldn't use the past as our ONLY source of information.

99

Normalize Rejuvenation

"The care, therefore, of every man's soul belongs unto himself."- John Locke

Because we're creatures of habit, most of us have systems in place that allow us to get done what needs to be done and still have at least a little time left over for ourselves…when life is "normal". However, sometimes life is not normal. Sometimes, things get very chaotic at work, kids get sick, we get sick, vacations happen, and weather issues like snow/ice close schools and make travel dangerous. Or, maybe your "normal" recently changed. Maybe you've started a degree or certification program, your child has started a new sport with a rigorous practice/game schedule, or your spouse took a new job that requires them to be away from home more than usual.

Impermanence is a fact of life. Everything is in a constant state of flux. To maintain our physical, mental, and emotional well-being through that change, we need to regularly check in with our recovery and rejuvenation strategies to ensure that 1) we're using them and 2) they are sufficient given our current circumstances.

What are your recovery and rejuvenation strategies? How do you ensure that you stay physically, mentally, and emotionally healthy? Do you exercise (e.g., workout videos, running, biking, skating, or walking)? Do you meditate or do yoga? Do you read, paint, sculpt, or practice magic? How often do you take advantage of those strategies? Do you have a regular schedule or try to fit the activities in whenever the calendar permits?

Today, take stock of your "normal" and commit to prioritizing and increasing how often you engage in at least one or two recovery/rejuvenation activities. Put these activities in your calendar and protect that time the same way you would with any other activity you thought was important…because they are important. Your health and well-being won't disappear overnight but will disappear without deliberate attention and effort. Make rejuvenation a normal, regular, and essential part of your "normal".

100

Is It Good or Bad? Stay Tuned....

-     A farmer's only horse ran away. Neighbor says, "That's horrible!" Farmer says, "Maybe."

-   The horse returns with additional horses from the surrounding area. Neighbor says, "That's terrific!" Farmer says, "Maybe."

-     While breaking one of the new horses, the farmer's son is badly injured. Neighbor says, "That's terrible!" Farmer says, "Maybe."

-     Representatives from the government come to conscript males for military duty; however, because of his injury, the farmer's son is not drafted and thus spared fighting in a bloody war. Neighbor says, "That's great!" Farmer says, "Maybe."

Parable from the ancient Chinese text, Huainanzi

It's easy to make quick judgments in the moment about whether things are good or bad, but how often are we later proven wrong?

Can you think of a time when your immediate impression of a situation was bad, but as you got more information, you realized what happened was actually good? Imagine that your alarm doesn't go off in the morning. You hate being rushed and hate being late to work even more, so this is a very bad thing. You quickly complete your morning ablutions, grab your stuff, and race to work. Once there, you realize that although you are late, everybody else is late, too. It turns out there was a wreck on the road that caused a lot of traffic. However, by the time you got to where the wreck had occurred, the traffic was already gone. So, by leaving later, you got to work at the same time everybody else did without the hassle of sitting in the traffic caused by the wreck. Now, the alarm not going off and the subsequent late departure seem like good things.

This type of situation happens all the time. Initially, we judge a situation to be good/bad, but when we find out more information, our assessment changes. This happens when we judge other people, too. We may see people doing something or hear them say something that we judge to be good/bad; however, after getting a little more information, we realize that our initial evaluation was incorrect. For example, maybe you turn a corner to see an adult grab a child's arm and yank the child violently toward them. Your initial impression is one of horror, anger, and indignation. Then, you see a bicycle careen by the adult and child at high speed, passing directly through the space occupied by the child just seconds before. With this new information, your impression of the adult's behavior will probably change.

Today, become aware of the value judgments you make, about others' behaviors/situations and your own. Then, remind yourself that your conclusion might be mistaken and that you might label the situation differently with more information. Be hesitant to assign the labels of good/bad, and be fully aware of how inaccurate, volatile, and easily changed those labels can be.

101

Stressed? Try This

"In the middle of difficulty lies opportunity." -Albert Einstein

"The greatest weapon against stress is our ability to choose one thought over another." -William James

Most of us regularly carry with us a great deal of stress. Right now, focus on the position of your shoulders. Chances are, they are closer to your ears than they should be. Try to relax your shoulders and see what happens. Did your shoulders drop as much as an inch or two from where they were before you relaxed them?

The symptoms of our stress plague us regularly. Beyond the tightness of our shoulders and the damage done to our teeth by constantly clenching our jaws, stress tires us out quickly, reduces our patience, increases our irritability, and significantly impacts our overall levels of well-being.

What are the indicators that let you know that you are stressed? Tune into your body and mind today and become aware of those moments when you are overly stressed. Then, attack the stress physically and mentally. Physically, roll your neck and shoulders, unclench your jaw, and take a long, deep breath. Mentally, shift your focus to something that triggers a positive emotion. Maybe it's a memory of a vacation or an image of your child or a joke you heard that made you laugh. Then, ask yourself how the situation you are currently in can be viewed as an opportunity, something to be thankful for, and ultimately beneficial to you.

By recognizing and targeting stress in the moment, we can quickly get our bodies and minds back to functioning at full capacity. We can boost our mood, improve our communication and interactions with others, and ensure that we are capable of our best in whatever situations we find ourselves in.

102

Rise Above the Storm

"When it is raining, we think that there is no sunshine. But if we fly high in an airplane and go through the clouds, we rediscover the sunshine again. We see that the sunshine is always there. In a time of anger or despair, our love is also still there. Our capacity to communicate, to forgive, and to be compassionate is still there." -Thich Nhat Hanh

B ad days are inevitable. These are the days when the adage, "If it can go wrong, it will," seems to operate in full force; when summoning to mind anything positive is a Herculean task; and when every undertaking seems destined to fail. These are days when affirmations and encouragement seem like empty platitudes and assault our senses as viscerally as nails on a chalkboard (for those old enough to remember chalkboards...).

On these days, it's important to remember that life is impermanent. Things will not stay the way they are in that moment. Like the quote above says, it's helpful to think of these days as stormy days. During stormy days, we may be buffeted unrelentingly by winds and soaked to the bone by rains, but the rain and wind don't last.

As importantly, we must remember that although the weather we are currently experiencing is turbulent, the blue sky and sunshine are still there. Immediate events might obscure them, but they haven't disappeared…which means they're still accessible if we transcend the stormy environment in which we are enveloped.

On those stormy days in your own life, take time to remember something that made you smile. This might be hard to do in the midst of the challenges you're facing, but it's possible…and it becomes easier to do with practice. Bring to mind a memory of a vacation, your child smiling or learning something new, or the moment you achieved a challenging goal you'd set for yourself. The positive emotions we feel when experiencing these memories can serve the same purpose as a plane on a stormy day. They can lift us above the chaos and allow us to experience beauty and peace… even if only for a few minutes. And on those difficult days, those few minutes can mean the difference between maintaining sanity and getting carted off to the loony bin.

103

The Process Matters

"Don't judge each day by the harvest you reap, but by the seeds that you plant."- Robert Louis Stevenson

Often in our society, the end is valued more than the process used to attain that end. This can be a problem for at least two reasons.

First, speed becomes more important than quality, so it's easy to focus more on simply getting something done than on getting something done well. Second, unethical behavior becomes much more likely to occur. This is the belief that "the end justifies the means."

For example, when grades in school become the only thing that are important...when grades are emphasized over the process used to attain those grades...cheating becomes much more prevalent. Also, when the end result is the only thing valued, businesses, as well as individuals, become more willing to cut corners and use any means at their disposal to get to the desired end state.

The next time you achieve a goal, evaluate yourself on the

process rather than the outcome. Assess how well you pursued the objective. Focus on the strategies you chose, the behaviors you engaged in, and the attitudes and mindsets you adopted along the way. If you're going to be proud, be proud not of the outcome, but of the process you used to reach the outcome.

104

Learn Something New

"An investment in knowledge pays the best interest." -Benjamin Franklin

"Knowledge is power." -Francis Bacon

Knowledge is a critical factor in our ability to navigate our environments successfully. In fact, our understanding of everything around us, from the most mundane interactions to the vast reaches of space, depends entirely on our knowledge. Knowledge determines and constrains what we think and how we perceive our surroundings.

For example, I can only conceive of what life might be like at dinner time in your house in terms of general knowledge of dinner time I've acquired over the years. I can create an idea in my mind of what dinner might be like in your house, but given my lack of knowledge about you and your circumstances (I obviously have none), my idea is likely very wrong. However, the more I learn about you, the more accurate my conceptualization of dinner time at your house would become. So, knowledge is essential for us to understand and predict literally everything accurately. Moreover, every time we acquire knowledge, the way we think about the world changes, even if only slightly.

Think about the understanding you have of the world around you. How accurate do you think you are? Is it possible that your current understanding of a situation at work, interactions with a friend or colleague, or some large and important world issue is wrong…or at the very least, incomplete?

Today, choose one situation you care about, personal or global, and think about…or even better, write down…how you currently view that situation. Then take time to learn one or two new things about the situation, things you didn't know about previously. Finally, assess how the additional knowledge changed how you understand the situation. The knowledge may have changed your mind completely, made you more confident in everything you already believed about the situation, or introduced doubt where before there was certainty. But whatever the change, the additional knowledge changed your understanding of the world. That's inevitable.

That's the power of knowledge.

105

Put Yourself in Timeout

"When I am completely by myself, entirely alone or during the night when I cannot sleep, it is on such occasions that my ideas flow best and most abundantly. Whence and how these ideas come I know not nor can I force them." -Wolfgang Amadeus Mozart

How much alone time do you get? Unfortunately, too many of us get very little. We wake up next to our spouses, interact with our children, work in a building with other people, come back home to our families, and go to sleep. In between, we go grocery shopping, cart our kids to various events, go to the gym, and engage in myriad activities involving being around other people. Relationships and interactions with other people are great and essential for us to be at our best. However, time to ourselves is valuable, too.

Alone time is important because it allows us time to reflect, learn, solve problems, and essentially hit the reset button on our mental and emotional states. When we are alone, we can assess past thoughts and behavior in order to understand better why we thought or acted the way we did; think critically and thoroughly about challenging issues we face and would like to address effectively; read books, listen to podcasts, watch Masterclasses, or utilize some other medium to learn new things; and reflect deeply on where we've been, where we currently are, and where we'd like to be in the future. Alone time also provides us with the space necessary to bring spiraling thoughts and emotions back under control.

Today, build alone time into your schedule at least once during the day. It doesn't have to be a huge amount of time, but it should be time that is protected, time when you have no other responsibilities. This is time devoted solely to you, for you to use however you find most valuable. Even 10-15 minutes a day of this designated time alone can work wonders for our attitudes, motivation, energy levels, clarity and understanding, and overall well-being.

106

What Do You Want?

Nobody likes to feel left out or ostracized by others. Nobody likes to feel like they've disappointed someone or let down people in their lives. So, sometimes… to avoid those feelings…we make choices we think will make other people happy rather than choices we think are right. We make decisions based on how we think others will think about us instead of our own core beliefs about the right thing to do.

Although considering how our actions will impact others can be a noble thing to do, we often find ourselves between a rock and a hard place. That is, we find ourselves struggling with a decision because Option A will result in one group of people happy and another group irritated, while Option B will result in the second group happy and the first group irritated. We find ourselves magnanimously trying to ensure that our actions result in the well-being of all involved, only to face the reality that, regardless of what we choose, someone somewhere will find a reason to criticize our actions. Therefore, since we can't please everybody, we should at least please ourselves.

Today, make sure that your choices and decisions satisfy you.

Make sure they align with your values, fit with your sense of right and wrong, and are easily defended in your own mind. Remember that pretty much any decision you make involving other people will result in some individuals happy and others upset. However, basing your decisions on your own sense of right and wrong allows you to be proud of your choices and minimize the likelihood of finding yourself in the upset group.

107

"Step Away" From Strong Emotions

"Don't allow your emotions to overpower your intelligence." -Morgan Freeman

I'm sure at some point you've noticed people who seem to exist constantly at the extremes of emotion. These people believe that every situation they encounter will have important, lasting, and dire consequences. Their realities are the epitome of exaggeration, and they revel in describing in detail the unique and abundant goodness or the abhorrent and dystopian badness associated with every encounter they have. These people can be exhausting.

Emotions, however, are contagious, so it's easy to get caught up in the emotional maelstrom these people carry with them wherever they go. Before we know it, we find ourselves swept up in their emotional current and, without really knowing how we got there, find ourselves nearly as distraught or jubilated as the people we're talking to. In these situations, self-awareness and self-regulation become critical to both our sanity and our ability to truly and rationally understand what is going on.

Today, if you find yourself caught up in an individual's or group's wave of emotion, recognize and tune into that emotional state as quickly as you can. Notice the change in your heart rate, breathing, and muscle tension. Notice the narrowing of your attention and the decreased ability to think broadly and rationally. Then, take a metaphorical (or literal) step away from what's going on. Take a deep breath; deliberately relax the muscles in your shoulders, neck, and jaw; and try to see the situation as clearly as possible. Think thoroughly, from all angles, about what is going on, so you gain as accurate an understanding of the situation as possible.

At the end of this assessment, your judgment will likely still be that things are "good" or "bad", but your understanding of the situation will be grounded much more firmly in reality than it was while being influenced and driven by dynamic, chaotic, and volatile emotions.

108

Which Brain Stories Are Holding You Back?

"I have been through some terrible things in my life, some which have actually happened." -Mark Twain

Probably the biggest obstacle to the commitment to and pursuit of new endeavors is fear.

Our brains don't like uncertainty or ambiguity. Our brains like complete and coherent stories and, when faced with incomplete information, tend to fill in that ambiguous space in ways that seem to make sense to us. This is the source of our fear.

When faced with the inherent uncertainty that goes along with beginning anything new, especially things that are big (e.g., starting a business), our brains try to alleviate that uncertainty by creating stories, and sometimes those stories involve us failing in countless, creative, and progressively worse ways.

To combat this fear, we must ground ourselves in reality, in the truth that exists in the here and the now, and remember two things. First, fear results from thoughts about things that might occur in the future. However, these thoughts aren't real; they're just thoughts...and like any thoughts, they will change. They won't last forever. No thought does.

Second, action immediately dispels fear. This is because fear exists in the future, while action exists in the present. Therefore, if we focus on tangible actions beneficial in the here and now, there is no room in our minds for fear.

The next time you notice feelings of fear or anxiety, remember that what you are afraid of is not real. It is only a fleeting, temporary, transient thought. It's just an imagination about the future you are creating in your mind. Remember, too, that any productive action you take will immediately alleviate the fear you experience.

109

What is "Success"?

"Look for small victories and build on that. Each small victory, even if it is just getting up five minutes earlier, gives you confidence. You realize that these little victories make you feel great, and you keep going. You realize that being paralyzed by fear of failure is worse than failure." -Arnold Schwarzenegger

How do you define "success"? Many of us only think about success in terms of achieving large, important things. With this mindset, we spend most of our time pursuing success and very little time experiencing success. However, success doesn't have to be tied to big, challenging goals. "Success" can often be something as simple as getting out of bed.

Allowing ourselves to feel successful on a regular basis helps us maintain motivation and energy levels, maximize our productivity, and keep a positive attitude and outlook on life. Today, consider two ways you might increase the success you experience in your life.

First, any big goal requires the completion of smaller behavioral tasks and consistent effort and perseverance when challenges arise

Rather than saving your feelings of success for completing the big goal, allow yourself to feel successful even when completing the smaller tasks that are essential to realizing your larger goal. Also, count as "success" the moments when you effectively overcome bad moods, lethargy, and doubt. Sometimes overcoming these internal challenges can be more difficult than any behavioral task we encounter.

Second, whether tied to a larger goal or not, recognize and appreciate anything you do well that is important and truly matters to you. This, again, might be behavioral, psychological, or emotional. For example, imagine there's a necessary but potentially challenging or uncomfortable conversation you need to have with a friend or spouse. Allow yourself to experience and celebrate success when you communicate your point clearly and articulately; manage your energy, emotions, and confidence effectively; and come away from the conversation with a sense that the issue you addressed has either been resolved completely or at least improved.

We need regular doses of success. So, today, choose to celebrate your successes. Celebrate those moments when you achieved something you set out to achieve...no matter how big or small.

110

Competition is Great! But Not for Judging Competence

"I am not competing with anyone other than myself. I want to be excellent at whatever I do." -Maya Angelou

Competing against other people can be a lot of fun. However, the result of a competition is a terrible measuring stick to use when evaluating our own competence.

Competition allows us to test our skills in situations very different from those we encounter in our regular, everyday training environments; exposes us to different strategies and techniques we may not have been aware of before; introduces us to new people; and provides opportunities to socialize in fun ways around activities that, hopefully, are enjoyable.

Although we obviously would like to win the competition, whether we win or lose provides us with only limited information about our competence because we can't control the other person. We can't control how much skill the other person or team has, nor can we control (or sometimes even know) how well the other person or team performed compared to their potential.

For example, in an ideal competitive scenario, both opponents give their best performances, and the more skilled competitor wins. However, this is rarely how things go. One opponent may have a bad day, a team may be missing a key player, or a referee or official may make (or fail to make) a call that changes the course of the game. There are simply too many variables that can affect the outcome of competition to be able to definitively say that, because we won (lost), we did well (or poorly). The only way to accurately judge our competence is to compare our current performances to our past performances.

So, the next time you catch yourself comparing yourself to others in an attempt to decide whether you are competent, stop and ask yourself whether you did better this time than last time. Judge your performance only in terms of your own skill level and potential.

Although competing against others can be a great thing to do for all the reasons listed above, competing against yourself...doing better than you have before...is a much more reliable and accurate way to assess our competence than the scoreboard at the end of a competition with others.

111

Combatting Temptation

"We gain the strength of the temptation we resist."- Ralph Waldo
Emerson

Temptations of all kinds surround us constantly. These temptations consist of things we know we shouldn't do or say and will, if succumbed to, negatively impact our lives in ways ranging from mild to catastrophic. For example, if you have a goal to lose weight and give in to the temptation to eat a muffin for breakfast, the date you set for achieving your target weight might need to get moved a little, but ultimately, the impact on your overall well-being will be small. However, if you struggle with alcohol addiction, succumbing to the temptation to drink can have tremendous consequences both personally (e.g., divorce; DUI) and professionally (e.g., loss of job).

Although we never know exactly when or where temptation will strike, we often have a very good idea. Using the diet example above, if we are going out to dinner with friends, it's likely someone will suggest dessert. If we realize this and plan for this possibility ahead of time, we can be ready to combat temptation should it occur.

But how can we combat temptation?

One strategy is not to put yourself in situations where temptation is likely to occur. Another strategy is to arm yourself ahead of time with something you can say to yourself that will remind you why you want to avoid the temptation. When using this strategy, stay away from self-talk that focuses on external rewards associated with the desired behavior. Instead, create self-talk that reminds you how avoiding temptation aligns with your core values and beliefs. A third strategy is to take some deep breaths to calm the inevitable anxiety that accompanies temptations when they arise.

Finally, you can practice all of this in your mind using mental imagery. For example, if you know you have a situation coming up where temptation is likely to be present, imagine that situation vividly in your mind and practice dealing with the physical and emotional feelings you'll encounter when the temptation is present using the three strategies discussed above. Regular practice makes deploying your strategies to resist temptation feel like second nature.

What are you trying to achieve? What temptations might you face that, if succumbed to, would hinder your ability to achieve what you'd like to achieve? When and where are you most likely to encounter those temptations? How can you employ the strategies and techniques above in ways that allow you to resist those temptations when they present themselves?

112

Cultivating No Opinion

"Too often we...enjoy the comfort of opinion without the discomfort of thought." -John F. Kennedy

When someone asks you, "What do you think?" how often do you say, "I don't know," or even "I don't care." It often seems like we're expected to have an opinion on everything. In fact, an opinion likely jumps into your mind immediately upon being asked what you think.

However, having an opinion on everything is exhausting, especially if you're going to support your opinion with facts. There are just too many things in the world for us to have a useful, evidence-based opinion about them all.

Today, when the opportunity presents itself for you to state your opinion on a topic you are only vaguely familiar with, or that doesn't really matter that much to you, try answering with either "I don't know" or "I don't care." This might be uncomfortable at first and require you to become okay with a certain level of vulnerability. However, giving yourself the freedom to ignore certain issues, to save your "mental RAM" for those issues you actually care about, is extremely liberating.

113

Fail-cede

"I can accept failure; everyone fails at something. But I can't accept not trying." -Michael Jordan

When we recognize that there is something that we would like to achieve, there are only three possible outcomes. We will succeed, fail, or "fail-cede".

When we realize that we want to accomplish, achieve, or obtain something, one possible outcome is that we succeed in our endeavors. We make a plan and do what's necessary for as long as necessary to obtain our desired objective.

Another possible outcome is that we fail, and there is really only one way to do that...to not even try, not even make an attempt to achieve what we'd like to achieve. This decision to not even begin pursuing your goals might stem from a lack of confidence, fear, or just plain laziness. Regardless of the reason, failing to put forth any effort toward obtaining what you've decided you'd like to have is truly the only kind of failure.

The last possible outcome is that we "fail-cede". This is when we pursue our objectives and goals to the best of our abilities and come up short. In the sense that we failed to achieve what we set out to achieve, we have failed. However, in the sense that throughout our pursuit we gained an abundance of useful knowledge and information about the goal we sought and about ourselves in general, we have succeeded. So, failing to obtain the end state you would have liked but developing, growing, and becoming better as a result of trying your best to achieve the desired outcome is "fail-ceding". We fail with regard to this one, specific goal but succeed in becoming better versions of ourselves.

So, the next time you decide that there is a goal you'd like to pursue, remind yourself that the only true failure comes when the decision you make is to quit before you even get started.

114

The Golden Mean

"Even nectar is poison if taken to excess." -Hindu Proverb

"Be moderate in order to taste the joys of life in abundance."
-Epicurus

"They are sick that surfeit with too much, as they that starve with nothing." -William Shakespeare

"Go big or go home!" "Do or die." "If a little's good, more's better."
At some point, you've probably heard, read, or even used one
or more of these phrases. However, living life in this "black or
white" way can be dangerous. Avoiding extremes and striving for
a moderate middle ground helps us maintain our relationships,
health, and sanity.

You've probably heard the phrase, "Everything in moderation."
This idea of not having, pursuing, partaking, or doing too little
or too much goes back thousands of years and spans nearly all
religions and philosophies, both Western and Eastern. From
Hindu texts and Confucius to Aristotle and Benjamin Franklin,
the wisdom of moderation has been preached loudly, clearly, and

consistently throughout the ages. There is even a quote carved in stone at the Temple of Delphi, which dates all the way back to between the 11th and 14th centuries BCE, that says, "All things in moderation."

The way Aristotle articulated this idea of moderation was in terms of the "Golden Mean". One example is the virtue of courage. According to Aristotle, courage can be thought of as the mean (i.e., average) of the two extremes of recklessness and cowardice. Another example is justice. This virtue can be conceptualized as the mean of the two extremes of strict legalism and nihilistic anarchy.

In our daily lives, this idea of moderation applies to the amount of work we do (mean between workaholic and slothful laziness), the food we eat (mean between fasting and gluttony), and the exercise we engage in (mean between strenuous exercise with no recovery time and no exercise whatsoever). Today, keep in mind this idea of moderation…the golden mean. Be attuned to your tendency to lean more toward one extreme or the other. Endeavor to strike a balance between extremes in all facets of your life.

115

It's the Walk Itself That's Important, Not the Destination

"I believe in process. I believe that having a really difficult process is more valuable than a good outcome." -Tina Fey

Have you ever achieved a challenging goal? If so, you began by identifying what you wanted to achieve. Then, you worked methodically and persistently to do what was necessary to accomplish your goal. These actions might have been behavioral (e.g., studying, writing), emotional (e.g., managing and regulating your disappointment when you encountered setbacks), interpersonal (e.g., effective communication with another person), or psychological (e.g., consistently maintaining confidence and motivation).

Then, finally, it happened…the moment came when your objective was realized. You made it! You accomplished your goal! You were very satisfied and proud of yourself…and you certainly should have been. The process you went through to achieve your goal was arduous, taxing, and demanding. However, it was also rewarding, gratifying, and satisfying. Really, if you stop to think about it, the process was much more of a reward than the ultimate achievement of the goal.

During the process of goal pursuit, we learn a great deal... about ourselves, others, different skills, and various areas. While pursuing our goal, we grow, develop, and improve as individuals in ways that would not have been possible without the vision we had in front of us every step of the way.

Today, keep in mind that your goal is simply the catalyst for personal growth. The rewards...the benefits of setting goals... actually come from the pursuit of the goal, not the achievement of the goal itself. Regardless of what stage of your goal pursuit you're in and whether you ultimately succeed or fail, you began the process of personal improvement the minute you put one foot in front of the other down the path toward your objective. And that improvement will continue with each additional step you take.

116

Relentlessly Pursue the Horizon

"One can choose to go back toward safety or forward toward growth. Growth must be chosen again and again; fear must be overcome again and again." –Abraham Maslow

The moment we believe that we've "arrived" is the moment that we begin our decline.

Change is constant. At no point in our lives are we standing still and maintaining a stationary existence. We are either progressing or retreating, improving or deteriorating, evolving or devolving.

This is why it's essential that we identify and continually strive to integrate our chosen values into all facets of our lives. Complacency can't be an option. Stagnation can't be acceptable. If we delude ourselves into thinking that we have reached our pinnacle, that we have arrived at our desired state of existence, we immediately begin our descent toward increased suffering and decreased well-being.

Life is a process. Every minute of every day is an opportunity to make choices and live out values in ways that ultimately benefit us and everybody we encounter. Each of those choices involves options that will move us forward or force us backward. At no point are we ever offered the option to stay exactly the way we are.

Today, embrace change. Recognize the minute-to-minute opportunities to increase well-being and value in your own life and the lives of those you love. Accept failure with a humility that allows you to learn and grow. Evaluate success in terms of controllable, repeatable actions and attitudes you adopted that led to that success. Seek advice and chances to move in directions different from those you have attempted in the past.

Pursue the horizon tirelessly and continue to "arrive" every day.

117

Rise and Excel

"Lose an hour in the morning, and you will spend all day looking for it." -Richard Whately

"The secret to getting ahead is getting started." -Mark Twain

How we begin our day often determines the trajectory of our day. The activities we choose, the mindset and attitudes we adopt, and the attentional priorities we decide upon all affect our productivity and well-being throughout the day.

Whether you're a morning person or not, you can create morning habits designed to ensure you begin your day mentally, physically, and emotionally in the most beneficial way. Today, think about your morning routine. When the alarm goes off, do you hit snooze? If so, stop doing that. Sleep is important, so decide what time you need to get out of bed and get as much uninterrupted sleep as you can before that time arrives.

Do you leave yourself enough time in the morning to do what you need to do without being rushed? If you have kids, do you schedule your time so there's a "cushion" there for when meltdowns occur? If not, you might consider waking up a little earlier and/or preparing the night before (e.g., make lunches, pack bags).

Do you wake up and immediately lose yourself mentally in the various tasks that await you throughout the day? If so, consider taking at least 5-10 minutes to meditate. Take a little time to set some intentions for your day, cultivate gratitude, or simply be in the present moment before propelling yourself into the chaotic and uncertain maelstrom of the future.

Do you take time to set your body up for success? If not, consider some gentle stretching and replacing no breakfast with a bar, smoothie, or shake that contains plenty of protein.

We can't control what will happen to us throughout our day, but we can absolutely control how we start our day. Today, begin your day in a way that will best prepare you for whatever it is life has up its sleeve.

118

Control Ourselves and Let Events Be What They Are

"Acceptance is the first step to overcoming the consequences of any misfortune."- William James

Regardless of how much we try to manufacture life just as we want it to be, events occur regularly that are out of our control. This is inevitable and unavoidable but doesn't have to be harmful. If we cultivate three skill sets, we can navigate these unpredictable life shifts in ways that are, ultimately, beneficial.

First, we need self-awareness. We need to be aware of what our expectations are, why we have those expectations, and how realistic those expectations are given our circumstances. We also need to be aware of when unforeseen events have hijacked our attention and emotions. Lastly, we need to be aware of how our thoughts and perceptions drive our emotions and attention.

Second, we need acceptance. Acceptance does not mean resignation. It simply means that we need to assess situations honestly and rationally. We need to divorce our immediate perceptions and knee-jerk reactions from the actual facts about the situation. This objective viewpoint allows us to figure out productive steps to deal with our situation.

Finally, we need self-regulation. Once we have some steps in mind we can take to handle whatever life has thrown at us effectively, we need self-regulation skills to implement those steps. We need the ability to direct our attention and thoughts to the most helpful places, manage our emotions in ways that allow those emotions to be assets and not liabilities, and regulate our physiology (e.g., heart rate, breathing, muscle tension) to maintain and utilize just the right amount of energy to handle our situation appropriately.

Today, practice self-awareness, acceptance, and self-regulation. Decide to become more aware of your thoughts, emotions, and actions. Make a deliberate effort to accept reality as it currently is. Develop your ability to manage and regulate your thinking, emotions, and physiology. The stronger these skill sets become, the more quickly life's uncertainties transform into life's opportunities.

119

Self-Awareness: Tune In to You

"Until you make the unconscious conscious, it will direct your life, and you will call it fate." -Carl Jung

To improve anything, we must be aware that improvement is necessary. This is true of any external life circumstances that happen upon us, but it is also true of ourselves. For example, if the way we are behaving, thinking, or interacting with others is making things worse, we need to be aware of that before we can make changes that allow improvement to occur.

Self-awareness can be difficult to develop, however, because we spend most of our time assessing our surroundings rather than ourselves. We spend a lot of time assessing and evaluating the world and other people around us, so we can understand better how to navigate our environments. Obviously, there is nothing wrong with a thorough understanding of our situations, but there IS something wrong with limiting our examination to ONLY our environments. Instead, we need to pay equal, if not more, attention to ourselves. How and to what we are paying attention? How do we perceive and interpret what happens around us, the emotions we experience and the reasons why we experience them, and the behaviors we choose throughout our day?

Today, take some time to turn your attention inward. See if you can tune into your thoughts and the emotions those thoughts are driving. Be aware of the meaning you assign to your circumstances and then deliberately try to perceive those situations differently. Notice your behaviors. Notice whether they are deliberately chosen, reactionary, or habitual as well as the extent to which your behaviors are effective.

Self-awareness can be a challenging resource to develop, but spending the time to develop it is well worth the effort. All personal growth and improvement depends on it.

120

Choose Through the Lens of Values

*"I am who I am today because of the choices I made yeste*rday."
-Eleanore Roosevelt

Sometimes making choices is easy (pizza vs. broccoli), and sometimes it's hard (pizza vs. cheesecake). Well, the second choice might not be that hard (cheesecake wins easily). Many times in life, though, we are faced with choices that are very difficult to make, either because we are forced to choose between two things we believe are equally good or equally bad. These are situations when understanding our values can be very helpful.

When faced with difficult decisions, the best question to ask is, "Which option fits best with my core values and beliefs?" Chances are, both decisions won't fit equally well. For example, if your choice is between lying on the couch watching football or playing a board game with your child, each option might seem like a good thing...but for very different reasons. When this happens, remembering our core values, the things we care most deeply about, can transform what initially was a challenging decision into a very easy one.

Today, when you're being pulled in two different directions and are having trouble figuring out "whether to go left or right", make sure that you're viewing the choice through the lens of your values. You might be surprised, once that shift in perspective happens, how quickly the right decision becomes abundantly clear.

121

Follow the 8-Fold Path

"A spiritual tradition is not a shallow stream in which one can wet one's feet and then beat a quick retreat to the shore. It is a mighty, tumultuous river which would rush through the entire landscape of one's life, and if one truly wishes to travel on it, one must be courageous enough to launch one's boat and head out for the depths."
-Bhikkhu Bodhi

Within the Buddhist tradition, there is something known as the 8-Fold Path. This path consists of eight things we can focus on to ensure ethical conduct, increase wisdom and mental discipline, and maximize our overall well-being. These eight things are all within our control and can be improved daily with deliberate, intentional practice. The eight components of the 8-Fold Path are: right understanding, right thought, right speech, right actions, right livelihood, right effort, right mindfulness, and right concentration.

Right understanding is having a thorough, accurate, unbiased understanding of reality.

Right thought is thought focused away from the self, toward others and their well-being, and on our interconnectedness with everything around us.

Right speech is composed of kind, honest, compassionate, considerate words designed to lift people up rather than tear them down and refrains from useless prattling and harmful gossip.

Right action refers to behaviors and choices that are peaceful, productive, and result in the enhancement of the common good.

Right livelihood refers to engaging in work that is beneficial and helpful for others.

Right effort is the continued determination to abolish harmful, unproductive ways of thinking and promote peaceful, beneficial, and productive ways of thinking.

Right mindfulness is diligent monitoring and acute awareness of mental, physical, and emotional factors influencing us throughout our day.

Right concentration refers to our ability to focus solely and exclusively on one thing without being distracted.

Today, try out the 8-Fold Path. Double-check the accuracy of your perceptions, shift your focus from yourself to others, speak to others in kind and compassionate ways, and behave in ways that benefit not only yourself but those around you. Spend your time working to better society and the lives of those within it, tune in to your thoughts regularly and adjust them quickly when you recognize they are heading in negative and unproductive directions, and practice focusing on one thing at a time. In this way, we can remain grounded, present, and confident that our thoughts and actions are increasing the well-being of ourselves and everyone around us.

122

Make Your Own Path

"Do not go where the path may lead, go instead where there is no path and leave a trail."- Ralph Waldo Emerson

There's a paradox we all must deal with starting very early in our lives. That is, we feel compelled, and are often encouraged to, go along with the crowd; however, in order for us to experience the individual growth and development we are uniquely capable of, we must separate from the crowd and interact with life on our own terms and in our own ways.

From the time we are children we are told explicitly and implicitly that we should behave the way the group behaves. We are pressured to conform to societal norms and led to believe that our success and well-being are tied to group acceptance and conformity. In some ways, this conformity is healthy because if something is working and beneficial for many people, it is often a pretty good thing for us, too. However, innovation is impossible if all that gets done is what has always been done.

The great advances that have occurred in our society…including art, science, and technology…have been made because someone ignored the norm, went against the grain, questioned the wisdom of the group, and challenged the status quo. Like the quote often erroneously attributed to Thomas Jefferson (but brilliant nonetheless) says, "If you want something you've never had, you have to be willing to do something you've never done."

How can you grow today? How can you leverage your unique talents and skills to forge a new path, to develop and improve yourself and the world around you in ways nobody has considered yet?

123

Stick With It

"Many of life's failures are people who did not realize how close they were to success when they gave up." -Thomas Edison

Finding things we'd like to do, and goals we'd like to accomplish...that's the easy part. Sticking with those goals long enough to achieve them...that's the challenge.

Have you ever found yourself bouncing from goal to goal? You see, read, or hear about something that gets you excited, decide that you want to do it, and then launch in the direction of that objective at a sprinter's pace. That pace can't be kept up for long, though, so not too far into the pursuit of the goal your motivation starts to wain and your progress begins to slow.

In precisely these moments, when what we really need to do is re-energize, remotivate, and re-engage, what we find ourselves actually doing is contemplating another goal, being pulled incessantly toward the next shiny thing. We give up on the first goal and begin pursuing the new goal. Too often, this same process is repeated...time after time and goal after goal...so we constantly strive and never achieve.

Curiosity and excitement are good; however, they must be tempered with self-control and tenacity. We need to be choosier about our goals and where we will expend our effort and energy. We need to keep our goal in the forefront of our minds and make the attitudes and efforts necessary to achieving that goal priorities in our lives. Only in this way can we avoid the cycle of beginning and abandoning the goals we set.

124

Choose Your Mood

"When you think things are bad, when you feel sour and blue, when you start to get mad... you should do what I do! Just tell yourself, Duckie, you're really quite lucky! Some people are much more... oh, ever so much more... oh, muchly much-much more unlucky than you!"
-Dr. Seuss

Bad moods are inevitable. We all experience them. However, a little bit of understanding about how moods affect us can sometimes be all we need to shift our mindset in a way that flips our bad mood 180 degrees.

The relationship between moods and perception is a complicated and circular one. When in a bad mood, we tend to more easily notice things that are wrong and perceive situations as bad. Similarly, when we focus on aspects of our environment we don't like and perceive our circumstances as undesirable, we generate bad moods.

The good news is that the reverse is also true. If we choose to direct our attention toward and express gratitude for those things going well in our lives, we can quickly transform a bad mood into a good mood. If we choose to view our situation...whatever it is...as an opportunity for some sort of growth and improvement, good moods emerge.

The next time you notice yourself in a bad mood, find something in your environment you are grateful for and put all of your attention on that one thing. As human beings, we can only focus on one thing at a time. Therefore, choosing to place 100% of your attention on this thing you're grateful for will force whatever you are unhappy about completely out of your awareness. Or, do an honest and thorough assessment of your situation...thoroughness being the key...and look for aspects of your situation that can be considered opportunities for betterment. Every situation has myriad ways it can be perceived. So, choose the way that will shift your mood in a more positive direction.

125

Pain is a Fertilizer

"Pain makes me grow. Growing is what I want. Therefore, for me pain is pleasure." -Arnold Schwarzenegger

Pain is not something most of us enjoy experiencing. Whether we're talking about physical, mental, or emotional pain, we try to avoid pain whenever possible. And when it's not possible, we try to reduce pain as quickly and easily as we can. Although completely understandable, this way of existing causes at least two problems.

The first problem is that many of the methods we choose to alleviate our pain are not healthy. Alcohol and drugs, both prescription and illicit, are common and dangerous ways we seek to eliminate pain. Overeating, gambling, and compulsive shopping are other addictive coping mechanisms we sometimes use to diminish the pain we feel.

We might also isolate ourselves from the world by erecting metaphorical...and sometimes actual...walls that will protect us from whatever is hurting us. Ironically, this isolation prevents us from receiving precisely what we most need when we're in pain, help and support from other people.

The second problem with prioritizing the avoidance and elimination of pain is that our efforts to extinguish and protect ourselves from pain blind us to the messages the pain is trying to communicate. If we are experiencing pain, something is wrong and needs to be addressed. Some sort of imbalance in our bodies or minds needs to be corrected. Numbing ourselves to pain prevents us from recognizing those problems and makes it impossible for us to address the cause of the pain.

Pain is not comfortable or fun, but it is essential for growth, development, and health. We should not avoid pain at all costs. In fact, just the opposite is true. We should tune in closely and immediately to our pain to better understand the source of the pain. Only in this way can we take active and productive steps to eliminate the pain in the short term, prevent the pain from returning in the future, and restore the natural balance in our minds and bodies.

126

Evaluate Yourself Using Your Own Measuring Stick

"The individual has always had to struggle to keep from being overwhelmed by the tribe. If you try it, you will be lonely often, and sometimes frightened. But no price is too high to pay for the privilege of owning yourself." -Friedrich Nietzsche

As social creatures, we constantly observe other people to see what they're doing and how they're doing it. We closely attend to how they behave and use what we see as a measuring stick for ourselves. Although this attention to others can be productive in some circumstances…for example, when trying to learn a new skill…it can be counterproductive in others.

Instead of setting the parameters for what is right and wrong by watching other people, we must create and adhere to our own standards and evaluate ourselves based on those ideals. We need to clarify our own values and beliefs and then align our thoughts and behaviors with those values and beliefs regardless of what others around us are doing or saying.

We can never control anybody else; we can only control ourselves. Moreover, people are volatile. Others, just like ourselves, have good days and bad days. Therefore, judging our performance, worth, or character in terms of what we witness others doing on any given day makes no sense. There is no accurate way to measure our progress in terms of other inconsistent, ever-changing people. The only way to truly evaluate our own thoughts, actions, and progress is in terms of the core values we hold and our own past performances.

So, today notice when you compare yourself to someone else, regardless of whether the comparison is favorable or not. Remember, if you are comparing yourself favorably, that person may just be having a bad day. If you're comparing yourself unfavorably, that person may be having an exceptionally good day. Either way, replace the measuring stick of the other person with your core values and beliefs and reevaluate yourself. Immediately, you will have a clearer and more accurate picture of how well you are meeting the standards that really matter…your own.

127

Because It's The Right Thing To Do

"You can always count on Americans to do the right thing – after they've tried everything else."- Winston Churchhill

In our society, we tend to be very transactional. If you do this for me, I'll do that for you. If you give me that, I'll give you this. When asked for a favor, we make decisions about granting that favor based on the likelihood that our benevolence will be reciprocated.

Unsurprisingly, our kids learn quickly to do the same thing. "You want a chore done?" they say. "What will you give me for doing it?" They quickly learn that their engagement at school is something that can be purchased for some candy. Even friendship becomes transactional. "If you do this thing for me, I'll be your friend."

Becoming extinct within our culture are people who do the right thing simply because it's the right thing to do. Rare is the person who sees someone in need and lends a hand for no other reason than that helping each other is what people should do. Even more extraordinary is the person who recognizes a need and provides support anonymously, neither seeking nor desiring any recognition whatsoever.

How often do you do a good deed without expecting anything in return? You simply do it because you know it will benefit someone else. How often, when someone asks for a favor or you recognize an opportunity to voluntarily provide support or help, does your mind quickly and readily do the math necessary to answer the question, "What's in it for me?"

Today, make it a point to do an anonymous good for someone else. Do something you know to be helpful with no possibility that the person/people you assist will ever know you were the one who helped. And do it for no other reason than because it's the right thing to do.

128

Train Your Mind

"The more we train our abilities, the stronger they become. The difference is that, unlike the body, when it comes to training the mind, there is no limit to how far we can go." -Dalai Lama

Every day we are bombarded by things associated with keeping our bodies in good shape. We see advertisements for gyms, health foods, supplements, healthy cooking strategies, and how to get great abs/legs/buns/biceps in only 10 minutes. Physical health is important, and we should absolutely take care of our bodies. However, our minds are equally, if not more, important for our well-being and success. So, why don't we spend as much time, effort, attention, and energy on improving our minds as we do our bodies?

To ensure that our minds are in the best shape they can be in, we need to focus on at least three areas: 1) What goes into our minds, 2) Exercising our minds, and 3) Allowing our minds to recover.

Just like what goes into our bodies affects our bodies' well-being, what goes into our minds affects our minds' well-being. Nonstop exposure to the nonsense spewed on social media is not helpful.

Instead, we should read books that make us think, watch shows that expand our minds, take a class in which we learn something new, and engage our friends and family in meaningful discussions about topics we believe are important.

We also need to make sure we regularly exercise our minds. Puzzles; pondering and discussing life's big questions; memorizing text from plays, poems, or books; doing creative things like painting, sculpting, or gardening; and writing fiction, nonfiction, or in a journal are all ways to exercise our minds.

Finally, we need to make sure our minds have sufficient time to recover. The best way to do this is to get plenty of sleep. During sleep, our brains flush out toxins and organize neuronal pathways based on what we've experienced while awake. This helps us remember more easily and learn more efficiently. In addition to getting plenty of sleep, we can help our minds recover by meditating and by reading fiction books we find entertaining.

To be at our best, we need both our bodies and our minds in tiptop shape. Today and over the next week or two, pay attention to what kinds of information enters your mind, deliberately set aside some time to exercise your mind, and allow time for your mind to recover. If you do, you'll quickly notice some big differences in your attention, memory, mental agility, and overall sense of well-being.

129

Principle of Charity

"How far you go in life depends on your being tender with the young, compassionate with the aged, sympathetic with the striving and tolerant of the weak and strong. Because someday in your life you will have been all of these." –George Washington Carver

There is no way to avoid people in our lives who irritate, upset, and aggravate us. It might be on the road while driving, in line at the grocery store, or in a movie theater, but wherever it is, people do things that we find annoying.

In these situations, we tend to be very quick to judge the person themselves based on their actions. We decide that they are bad people because of the behaviors we see. However, it's important to remember in these situations that we only have a very small amount of information.

All we know about this person we're so angry at is what we see in this moment. What we don't know is anything else at all about their life. It's possible this person just received a scary diagnosis from the doctor, has been up the last three nights in a row with a sick baby, or was just laid off from one of the three jobs they work daily to make ends meet. The truth is that we really know nothing about this person's life, so making accurate character judgments is not only next to impossible, but also not fair.

The principle of charity refers to giving people the benefit of the doubt, assuming a priori that they are honestly and truthfully trying their best to do the right thing. The next time you encounter someone whose behavior makes your blood boil, try changing your viewpoint and apply the principle of charity.

None of us are perfect. We make mistakes, too. Today, choose to decrease your stress by increasing your compassion.

130

Is Your Worrying Working?

"That the birds of worry and care fly over your head, this you cannot change, but that they build nests in your hair, this you can prevent."
-Chinese Proverb

Unless you are an accomplished and practiced Buddhist monk, you probably spend a significant amount of time worrying. Worry is defined by author Oliver Berkman as "the repetitious experience of a mind attempting to generate a feeling of security about the future, failing, and then trying again and again and again – as if the very effort of worrying might somehow help forestall disaster." The truth is, though, that that sense of security and certainty about the future is impossible. We can't know the future.

As soon as we accept the fact that the future is unknowable and that any sense of certainty is an illusion, we can bring our minds back to the present, back to the only time and place when concrete steps can be taken to mold the future into what you would like it to be. In the here and now is when the future is created. Our actions in this present moment determine the future we experience.

So, today, notice when you are lost in worry about the future and use a few deep breaths to bring your mind back to the present. Once grounded in the present moment, ask yourself what future you would like to experience and what you can do right now to help usher that future into existence. You will be surprised at how quickly the debilitating worry leaves your mind and body once you rescue your mind from the maelstrom of uncertainty that is the future and direct your attention to actionable things you can do in the present moment.

131

Resilience: Get It Before You Need It

"You reach inside yourself to discover your personal resources, and what it takes to match them to the challenge." Arnold Palmer

When bad things happen, we need to be able to handle those things effectively in the moment and recover from those things quickly once life returns to normal. That is, we need to be resilient.

How resilient we are depends on the amount and strength of resources we have available to use. The more resources we have, the better we are able to deal with and recover from life's challenges. These resources can be physical, social, financial, psychological, spiritual…there are many different types of resources. However, for those resources to be helpful to us, they must already be in place when adversity strikes. So, how do we make sure we have access to these resources?

The good news is that resources can be developed, and a great time to develop them is before we need them. For example, while life is cruising along in its normal way, develop physical resources by eating healthily, exercising regularly, and getting enough sleep; social resources by prioritizing quality time with friends and family; financial resources by making and sticking to a budget; and psychological resources by tuning into and managing your thoughts, questioning the accuracy of your perceptions, and deliberately choosing helpful and productive ways to interpret every situation you're in.

What resources can you develop today? What actions can you take to regularly grow and improve the resources you have at your disposal, the resources that will be essential when life's inevitable challenges arise?

132

Everybody Does the Best They Can

"Ignorance, the root and stem of all evil." Plato

"All I know is that my life is better when I assume that people are doing their best. It keeps me out of judgment and lets me focus on what is, and not what should or could be." Brené Brown

Rarely does a day go by when we don't notice somebody doing something we think is wrong. It might be something they say or the way they act or the reasoning they use to justify something going on in the world. Whatever it is, the conclusion we draw is that these people are wrong.

But we don't stop there.

We also assign a reason for why these people are wrong, and that reason is often that they are bad people. They are fundamentally flawed in some way. That is, we attribute their bad behavior to stable personality characteristics rather than situational influences that may be salient in that moment.

However, according to many philosophers dating all the way back to Socrates, people never try to do wrong. Instead, they are always acting in ways that, given their current knowledge and circumstances, they believe are best.

The next time you see someone doing or saying something you disagree with, give that person the benefit of the doubt. Assume that the person is doing what they truly think is best in that moment. Then, try to see the situation from that person's perspective. Put yourself in their shoes. This may not change whether you think what they're doing is right or wrong, but it will give you more insight into why they're doing what they're doing, whether you agree with their reasoning or not. With this new perspective, we can choose much more compassionate and productive ways of dealing with the people we meet every day.

133

We Are Not Interchangeable Cogs in a Machine

"The person who follows the crowd will usually go no further than the crowd. The person who walks alone is likely to find himself in places no one has ever seen before." -Albert Einstein

"I find that the very things that I get criticized for, which is usually being different and just doing my own thing and just being original, is the very thing that's making me successful." -Shania Twain

Throughout our lives, we experience a strong pull to conform to others. Finding ourselves as outliers in terms of our thoughts, beliefs, and behaviors can be extremely stressful and can cause us to deny our true thoughts, feeling, and perceptions in an effort to fit in with the group. This phenomenon has been demonstrated countless times by researchers but is so common that there are none among us who can honestly say they have not made certain decisions simply to avoid being singled out from the crowd.

However, as useful as group cohesion and agreement can be in some situations, we are unique. Each of us has our own passions, skills, talents, dreams, and experiences that separate us from other people in meaningful ways. Nobody perceives or understands the world exactly like you do. Nobody has insight into anything going on exactly like you do. Therefore, to ensure that we realize our full potentials, we need to be willing to embrace our uniqueness. We need to be willing to express opinions and behave in ways that are different from what "everybody else" is doing.

Today, notice the strong temptation you feel to go along with the status quo. Recognize the hesitation and anxiety, however small it might be, you feel when you consider going against the norm, stepping outside of "how things are done." Then, remind yourself of the talents and perspectives that only you can bring, the knowledge and experience that only you have. Only then, only after considering the strengths and assets you bring to the table, are you ready to decide whether to walk the well-beaten path or blaze your own trail.

134

Your Default Mode

"[Mindfulness] is the antidote to mind wandering, it's paying attention to our present moment experience without editorializing or reacting to it." -Amishi Jha

Sometime today, guaranteed, you will suddenly realize that you have been lost in thought. We call this daydreaming or mind wandering, and we often think about these two things as being counterproductive...and sometimes they are. However, each is the result of the brain doing what the brain seems wired to do most easily and most often.

Over the last twenty years or so, neuroscientists have identified and researched extensively something called the default-mode network. This is a network of neurons located in specific areas of the brain that appears to be continually "on" unless we intentionally focus our attention on external, goal-directed behavior. That is, unless we deliberately tune into our surroundings, the brain's default-mode network is active. This is why we spend so much time dwelling on things that occurred in the past and creating stories about what might occur in the future. This is the type of thinking the default mode network does naturally.

So, the next time you berate yourself for losing your focus and becoming distracted, cut yourself some slack. Chances are, it's just your brain doing what it was designed to do. This doesn't mean, however, that we are at the mercy of our default-mode networks. Research has shown that mindfulness training can help quiet the default-mode network and help us get much better at consistently directing, sustaining, and regaining attention.

Today, tune into when your default-mode network is activated. Notice how you can be intently focused on a task one minute and totally lost in thoughts completely unrelated to the task the next minute. To enhance your ability to quiet the default-mode network, regularly engage in mindfulness meditation. It might take a while, but with practice, you will be able to sustain attention longer, recognize distractions more quickly, and regain your focus more efficiently.

135

Things Are Not Always What They Appear To Be

"Do not judge, and you will never be mistaken."- Jean-Jacque Rousseau

As we walk through the world, we notice others' behaviors, we hear others' words, and we form opinions based on those things we see and hear. But, are your opinions true? Are the conclusions you draw after simply seeing or hearing someone's actions and words accurate?

Jodi Picoult writes, "Who we are is about not what we do, but why we tell ourselves we do it." That is, the motivation behind what we do and say is really what's important, not the speech and behavior themselves. For example, if you see someone hand money to a homeless person, you might think to yourself that you've just witness a selfless act. However, what if the reason the person gave money was out of fear of being harmed or as a down payment for drugs or out of a sense of guilt because they are responsible for the person being homeless in the first place?

The point is that the behavior looks the same regardless of whether the person's motivation is benevolent or sinister. It's the reason for the behavior that determines what we think about the behavior and the person doing the behaving.

Today, notice how often you jump to conclusions about people's motivations, their rationales for acting and speaking in the ways they do. How sure are you that you're correct? What other motivations or rationales might exist for the behavior you just witnessed?

Whether we judge the behavior as good or bad depends on the motivation we assign to the person doing the behaving…and most of the time, that motivation is impossible for us to be sure of. So, how about giving people the benefit of the doubt?

136

A Mirror is the Best Measurement Tool

Most of us spend a great deal of time judging ourselves by comparing ourselves to other people. We decide how well we're dressed by comparing our clothing choices to the outfits of others at the event. We judge how well we parent by comparing our behaviors and interactions with our kids to those of other parents. We evaluate how good we are at our job by how we believe we measure up to others in our office or in our field. Often, it seems like our lives are one big series of comparisons.

The problem with using other people as measuring sticks for what "right" looks like is that other people are not consistent. You have no idea whether they are excelling or having a bad day... there's no way for you to know. For example, that outfit you admire at a party might be a gift from the person's spouse and is being worn only to avoid hurting the spouse's feelings. That parent you see yelling in a child's face and to whom you are comparing yourself favorably might have just been fired or is on medication that impacts their emotional state. We simply don't know.

Understanding the extent to which we are competent and effective in our environments is essential. However, rather than using comparisons with others to evaluate our competence, we need to use comparisons to ourselves. Judge your wardrobe by well your clothes fit your taste, style, and value preferences, not by how other people dress. Parent in ways that are congruent with your values and what you think is important for your child, your family, and society at large, not by how other parents behave with their children. And, determine your effectiveness at your job, your hobby, the pursuit of your goals…whatever…by your past performances, by whether you are better today than you were yesterday, not by how your skills and abilities compare to others.

Judge yourself in terms of yourself. Any other measuring stick will be unpredictable, inconsistent, stressful, and..ultimately… useless.

137

Beware of Certainty

"Ignorance more frequently begets confidence than does knowledge: it is those who know little, not those who know much, who so positively assert that this or that problem will never be solved by science."
-Charles Darwin

"I believe in intuitions and inspirations...I sometimes FEEL that I am right. I do not KNOW that I am." -Albert Einstein

We've all been there...to the promised land...certainty! We know for SURE! There is no doubt in our minds that we are correct and understand completely. It's definitely a great feeling. Who likes doubt and uncertainty, vagueness and ambiguity? Not very many people. However, instead of relief, a sense of certainty should raise big, giant red flags all around us. When certainty arises, we should immediately be skeptical and ask ourselves what we're missing.

This is because the world is complex, and humans are fundamentally limited in our cognitive and perceptual abilities. We are simply incapable of perceiving everything around us or fully understanding all that happens to find its way into our consciousness. Therefore, humility about what we know and how well we understand is essential.

Throughout history, many smart people, going all the way back to Socrates, have stated various versions of this quote often attributed to Socrates, Plato, or Aristotle, "The more I know, the more I know I know nothing." That is, as we learn more and more about our environments and the world in which we live, we begin to realize that things are much bigger and more complicated than we are capable of grasping fully. We start to see the nuances and situational interdependences we encounter in nature and in everyday life that defy one's ability to truly recognize, let alone comprehend, all of the relevant and important components and relationships.

The next time you find yourself certain of something, ask yourself, "What am I missing?" Because you're human, there is absolutely information that you are not aware of. Cognitive biases are affecting how you're interpreting the information you have access to, and your limited knowledge, abilities, and past experiences are influencing the options you see available and which of those options make the most sense to you.

So, instead of certainty being the desired end state, let it be a cue for curiosity. Let your sense of certainty propel you toward information-gathering and outside-the-box thinking. Let it trigger a growth mindset that opens you up to new possibilities and insights. You'll be surprised and humbled by how much you don't know.

138

Create a New Story

"The world is full of magic things, patiently waiting for our senses to grow sharper." -W.B. Yeats

Too often we tend to adopt the same predictable, narrow, unimaginative ways of perceiving our environments. We gravitate toward these same viewpoints for a few reasons.

First, the viewpoints are familiar. Whatever situation we're in, we tend to see and experience what's going on in the same ways we have in the past.

Second, our usual perspectives are easy. Habits are not only formed around behaviors; they are also formed around thoughts, perceptions, and emotions. So, if we regularly find ourselves viewing situations or people in certain ways, it is much easier for us to maintain those perceptions in the future because of the perceptual habits we've developed.

Third, when we label something as a problem, our attention tends to narrow and focus directly on the factors we believe are contributing to that problem. We tend to block out the bigger picture and, instead, zero in on only the factors we've immediately identified as being responsible for our predicament.

Whether we allow our perceptions to materialize out of familiarity, ease, or narrowed attention, we fail to consider a lot of available information that might significantly improve our understanding of our circumstances. The next time you notice yourself falling into a rote perception of your environment, stop and ask what you might be missing. Challenge yourself to come up with an alternative story to the one you automatically created in your mind.

The world is a complicated and nuanced place. Let's develop an awareness and thinking style that is up to the task of navigating it successfully.

139

It's Not About Me

"Selfless action is a source of strength." -Mahatma Gandhi

If you want to maximize your own happiness and well-being, pay more attention to other people than to yourself.

The scientific literature…and the religious and philosophical literature…make it abundantly clear that we tend to feel better when we focus the vast majority of our attention on other people rather than on ourselves. We can boost our moods and happiness levels very simply and quickly through small, seemingly inconsequential interactions with others. Just a short exchange with a coworker in the hall or the barista at a coffee shop can enhance our overall sense of well-being.

This phenomenon works when things are going well, but it works even better when things are going badly. When you're feeling down or even outright miserable, avoid the natural tendency to retreat inside yourself and, instead, look for someone you can talk to. Better yet, look for someone you can help. Selfless behavior can work wonders on those dreary, melancholy moods and the stress and anxiety that so frequently impact all of us from time to time.

Today, take stock of your overall mood and the types of thoughts and emotions you're experiencing. Next, engage in conversation with someone about themselves or help someone…even in just a very small way. Hold a door, bring a cup of coffee, or smile and wave. Then, check in with your mood, thoughts, and emotions again. Chances are, you'll see a positive shift in your sense of happiness and well-being.

140

Every Choice Changes Us

"We are our choices." -Jean-Paul Sartre

Everything in this life is impermanent and in a constant state of flux, including ourselves. Every decision we make alters us in some way. Sometimes we change a little, and sometimes we change a lot. Sometimes we change for the worse and sometimes for the better. What we will never do, however, is stay the same.

Understanding and appreciating this inevitable change is essential if we want our decisions to be ones that will lead to positive, productive outcomes. However, understanding the inevitability of change by itself is not enough. We also need wisdom.

Wisdom is the culmination of all our knowledge and experience. With wisdom comes the ability to understand our circumstances clearly, honestly, and thoroughly and to act in the best, most appropriate manner.

Today, notice the decisions you make and how frequently you

make them. Every one of those decisions is a chance to move yourself forward or backward. Remember, change is going to happen. So, take control of that change by making sure your choices are intentionally made and move you in the direction you want to go.

141

Don't Be A Zombie

"Life can be found only in the present moment. The past is gone, the future is not yet here, and if we do not go back to ourselves in the present moment, we cannot be in touch with life." -Thich Nhat Hanh

Zombies take many forms in classic horror stories. However, zombies also take a very recognizable form right here in everyday reality. Unfortunately, that form is too often the same form we see when we look into the mirror.

Zombies are most often described as beings that are "undead". That is, they are "alive" in the sense that they are perceiving and reacting to the world around them, but they are "dead" in the sense that they are not conscious...the "lights are not really on."

How many times have you navigated your way down a hallway, sidewalk, or road only to realize that you really have no recollection of how you made it from where you were to where you are? In these situations, you were obviously perceiving the environment around you and reacting to what you perceived because you didn't crash into the wall, another person, or another car. However, you weren't truly aware of what you perceived because few, if any, of the things you encountered along the way actually made it into your conscious awareness.

Reality only exists in the here and now. So, the present moment is the only moment in which we can be really conscious, really connected, and truly aware of our reality. The present moment is the only place where zombies can be resurrected and turned back into humans.

Today, notice when you are in "zombie-mode". Notice when you are tuned out to what is around you, when you are lost in the past or fantasizing about the future. Then, as soon as you recognize your disconnection with the present moment, bring your focus back to the here and now. Become consciously aware of your physical, mental, and emotional states of being. Send your zombie back to the grave where it belongs.

142

Accept What Is

"Happiness can only exist in acceptance." -George Orwell

The first step to handling life's challenges successfully is to accept that the challenges exist and that change is inevitable.

At first glance, this may seem obvious. However, too often, we find ourselves fighting against reality by attempting to ignore or deny that challenges are a normal part of life and that nothing in this universe is permanent. We try our best to convince ourselves that our problems aren't really problems, that what we're facing isn't that big a deal, or that the way things are is the way things will always be.

Acceptance is about meeting reality where it is, whether pleasant or unpleasant. It is about acknowledging things exactly as they are in an honest and straightforward way. It is about embracing the paradox that although change itself is completely predictable, we can never accurately predict what that change will be or when and to what extent the change will occur.

What aspects of your life do you need to accept? What parts of your reality are you trying to ignore or gloss over? What parts of your life are you taking for granted? What parts of your life are you assuming will stay the same?

Today, do an honest and thorough assessment of your situation. Then, accept things as they currently are. Acknowledge reality as it exists right now, in this moment. Until you do, improvement and well-being will prove very elusive.

143

Time...Is It Creating or Destroying?

"He who every morning plans the transactions of that day and follows that plan carries a thread that will guide him through the labyrinth of the most busy life." -Victor Hugo

"You must vie with time's swiftness in the speed of using it, and, as from a torrent that rushes by and will not always flow, you must drink quickly." -Seneca

"You may delay, but time will not." -Benjamin Franklin

Time, in some ways, is like fire. Left on its own, with no attention paid or boundaries enforced, fire can consume and destroy everything it touches. However, when deliberately harnessed, fire can be used for productive and helpful purposes. For example, fire can provide heat for survival, fuel and energy for propulsion (e.g., trains, boats), and the ability to quickly and safely clear away overgrown plants and trees.

In the same way, time...when ignored and taken for granted, can quickly erode opportunities, disintegrate relationships, and destroy any chance for meaningful growth or improvement. When time is used wisely, however, there are no bounds to the creations, improvements, and goodness that can manifest.

Today, take a close look at your relationship with time. Are you using it, or is it using you? How might you make more intentional use of the time you are afforded? Time can be a resource or a liability... it's your choice.

144

Abolish Secrets

"Live in the open." Auguste Comte

"For nothing is secret, that shall not be made manifest; neither any thing hid, that shall not be known and come to light."
Jesus; Luke 8:17

We all do things and have aspects of our lives that we're not particularly proud of. Maybe we're easily triggered by life's events and say things or make choices that, in retrospect, we wish we hadn't. Or, maybe we tend to speak and act rashly and impulsively. Although not enjoyable, occasional occurrences of these types of things are natural and unavoidable. Two ways to handle these situations are to 1) Hide them or 2) Ignore them and pretend they didn't happen. Neither choice is as effective, however, as simply acknowledging the mistakes we make and asking forgiveness from whomever we may have inadvertently harmed with our words or actions.

However, there are other times when we make a conscious decision to do something we know we shouldn't and intentionally take elaborate steps to keep anyone from knowing what we've done. In these situations, two big problems arise. First, although we might successfully keep what we've done secret for a time, the truth...sooner or later...tends to come out. And when it does, the damage to your reputation and your relationships can be catastrophic. Second, even if the secret remains a secret, YOU know what you've done. You know that what you did was something you shouldn't have, so there will be inevitable and ever-present guilt that can make life truly miserable.

The best thing we can do is endeavor to live our lives as honestly and truthfully as we can. This helps us avoid choices and behaviors that cause the type of shame that leads to trying to keep that behavior secret. Today, live life in a way that produces no guilt. Make choices and use words you feel no need to retract and have no problem with anybody else knowing. Live openly and truthfully, and model the behavior you'd like your kids to emulate.

The rewards of living guilt-free, of being able to walk with your held high, of knowing that you have acted honorably and honestly are absolutely worth the effort.

145

Keep Commitments But Be Open to the Power of "No"

"I can give you a six-word formula for success: Think things through, then follow through." - Eddie Rickenbacker

"The oldest, shortest words – 'yes' and 'no' – are the ones which require the most thought." -Pythagoras

We live in a society that values "busy"…so much so that we often feel compelled to recount exactly how busy we've been anytime we're asked the question, "How are you doing?" Most of us, when faced with that question, recite a laundry list of our activities, despite the glazed look that frequently comes over our interlocutor's eyes. We do this because we feel compelled to justify our existence. Wasted time in our society is frowned upon, so any downtime spent must be vehemently defended with detailed explanations of the myriad activities that have depleted our energy to the point where we had no other option but to recharge.

Because of the way Americans deify "busy", we often feel

pressured to accept responsibilities we really don't have time for and make commitments we know will be nearly impossible to keep. Sometimes this happens because we seek out too many undertakings and sometimes because we say "yes" to too many requests from others. Both possibilities put us in essentially the same predicament, and we find ourselves committed to things we either don't have time to do or don't really want to do.

Cultivating trust, acting responsibly, and demonstrating dependability are virtuous actions that are important for our personal and professional relationships. Therefore, when a commitment is made, following through on that commitment is the virtuous thing to do, the thing that will maintain and even strengthen your relationships with other people and organizations. However, whether we should have made the commitment at all is really the question we should ask ourselves more often than we do.

Today, take stock of your current commitments. How much time do you spend on commitments you would rather not have? What is the opportunity cost for fulfilling these commitments? That is, what are you missing out on doing because you're fulfilling these commitments instead? Which commitments are one-time commitments, and which are commitments that could go on indefinitely? Can you commit to not committing again to the one-time commitments? Is there a way to honorably extract yourself from ongoing commitments?

Staying engaged in society, contributing to causes, helping others, and furthering our own growth and development are all good things. However, we must also recognize that there are only 24 hours in a day, we are only human beings, and our overall well-being is threatened when we overcommit. So, if you've said "yes" to a commitment, fulfill that commitment to the best of your ability. That's absolutely the right thing to do. However, if you're considering saying "yes" to more commitments when you know your dance card is already full, consider saying "no" instead. You might be surprised at the unforeseen benefits you, your friends, your family, and possibly even the person you were about to commit to experience as a result of simply saying "no".

146

Happiness Drives Success…Not the Other Way Around

"Your success and happiness lies in you. Resolve to keep happy, and your joy and you shall form an invincible host against difficulties."
-Helen Keller

How many times have you thought to yourself, "As soon as I get this thing/reach this goal/attain this objective, I'll be happy/satisfied/able to relax?" This type of thinking is very common in our society…that we need to have something we don't currently have in order to be happy. However, this thinking is misleading at best and completely wrong at worst.

This way of thinking is misleading because, although it is absolutely true that we experience a boost in happiness and satisfaction when we achieve a goal that we've worked long and hard to achieve, it is also true that the happiness and satisfaction boost is short-lived. This experience of quickly returning to the same state of happiness we had prior to achieving the goal is known as hedonic adaptation, or the hedonic treadmill.

Beyond being simply misleading, research has actually shown that this way of thinking may be fundamentally wrong. That is, the causal direction could work the other way around. When we regularly experience positive emotions, our attentional awareness tends to open up, and we interact with our environments in fuller and more nuanced ways. This expanded attention and enhanced environmental interaction set conditions for developing the social, intellectual, psychological, and physical resources essential for success in all facets of our lives.

So, instead of thinking about happiness and positivity as resulting from achievement, think of them as factors that boost your chances of achieving in the first place. Today, increase the chances of succeeding by cultivating positive emotions. Adopt an optimistic mindset, choose to notice and appreciate what you have instead of what you don't, and express gratitude freely and liberally. Not only will your well-being and quality of life improve, but you'll make it more likely that the goals you've set will ultimately be achieved.

147

Have the Tough Conversations

"Sunlight is said to be the best of disinfectants."- Supreme Court
Justice Louis Brandeis

Sometimes challenging conversations are necessary. These are conversations with others that are guaranteed to trigger intense emotions and/or strong resistance, but the subject matter is important enough that it needs to be brought up regardless of the discomfort involved for either person. When these situations arise, our tendency is often to rationalize or justify why it's okay to put off or postpone the conversation. We come up with increasingly creative reasons why it's actually a good thing that we aren't having the conversation.

In these situations, situations in which something important really needs to be addressed but we continuously avoid initiating that discussion, we need to look honestly at why we are procrastinating, why we are so hesitant to do what we believe needs to be done. Chances are, it's primarily because of uncomfortable emotions and suffering we, ourselves, expect to experience rather than anything having to do with the other person. Viewed through this lens, postponing and continuing to rationalize our avoidance of the conversation is actually an act of selfishness.

For example, if you believe someone close to you is developing a substance abuse problem, bringing up that sensitive subject can create a very uncomfortable situation for ourselves. However, addressing a substance abuse problem sooner than later can potentially save that individual a huge amount of pain and undesirable consequences. So, any avoidance of the discussion on our part is clearly selfish. What's best for our loved one is for us to push through our worry, embarrassment, and discomfort and have the conversation for their sake.

Are there any challenging conversations you're avoiding? If so, why are you avoiding the discussion? If it's something important, why are you putting it off? Stop procrastinating. Stop being selfish. Deal with the issue…whatever it is…head on.

148

Embrace Entropy

"Change is the law of life and those who look only to the past or present are certain to miss the future." -John F. Kennedy

"Whosoever desires constant success must change his conduct with the times." -Niccolo Machiavelli

Nothing stays the same. Change is constantly occurring, and it's occurring in a predictable way: from order to disorder. Entropy is defined as the amount of disorder present in a system...systems like our bodies. As time passes, entropy within the system gets higher, and disorder becomes more prevalent. This is evidenced by cells regenerating less efficiently, bones becoming less dense, and muscles losing elasticity. These changes are normal, natural, and predictable. This is simply the reality of nature.

Similarly, change in our everyday lives is inevitable as well. Our relationships, priorities, physical and mental abilities, wisdom, compassion, communication style and skill, and many more things all change. These changes are also normal, natural, and to be expected.

Understanding that change is a natural and unavoidable part of life gives us an advantage, because we can plan ahead. We might be making a lot of money now, but we can plan for a time when… because of retirement, injury, or some other reason…we aren't making as much money. Our kids might be in elementary school now, but we can plan for the time when they are in high school, college, and beyond. Accepting the inevitability of change gives us an edge. We don't have to be held back by the misconception that how things are is how things will always be. Instead, we can acknowledge and truly accept that things will be different tomorrow than they are today and plan accordingly.

While planning, however, it's important that we adapt at the same pace at which change is occurring. That is, we don't want to be overzealous and adjust too quickly or overly aloof and conservative and adjust too slowly.

Change happens gradually and, as such, can be difficult to detect. Today, compare your life now to your life one, five, and ten years ago. Where were you living? What were you doing for a living? Who were your close friends, and how often did you see and talk to them? What were your favorite foods? How often did you exercise? Were you in a relationship? If in a relationship with the same person, how would you rate that relationship on a scale of 1-10 at each time period? How often did you go out to socialize? What shows did you watch? What types of books did you read? If you weren't aware of it before, asking yourself these types of questions will quickly bring the amount of change you've experienced into sharp focus.

Change isn't bad…it just is. Rather than denying it or ignoring it or fighting it, plan for it.

149

Let Go of Entitlement and Embrace Gratitude

"What separates privilege from entitlement is gratitude."- Brené Brown

Have you ever found yourself resentful because you didn't get something you felt you deserved? Of course, you have; we all have. By the same token, we've all experienced the satisfaction that comes from receiving what we felt we deserved. It could be a bonus or promotion at work, congratulations or recognition for something you've done, or even something as simple as a birthday card from a friend or family member. If we feel we deserve it, then we're satisfied when we get it and resentful, upset, and angry when we don't.

However, consider a different perspective.

Imagine the same situations described above, but instead of feeling like you deserved them, imagine that you felt no sense of entitlement whatsoever. In that scenario, how would feel if you got the promotion/bonus, recognition, or card? How would you feel if you didn't?

Feeling entitled, like we deserve something, robs us of any possibility of feeling joy if something good happens and guarantees suffering if it doesn't. When we receive what we believe we deserve, we feel no happiness, joy, or excitement; we simply feel content. Conversely, when we don't get what we believe we deserve, we are guaranteed to be upset because we perceive ourselves to have been mistreated. We become indignant, resentful, and angry. With entitlement, there is no upside, only a downside.

However, if we avoid that feeling of entitlement, we open ourselves up to experience joy, surprise, happiness, and gratitude. We create the possibility for pleasant surprise and appreciation for what we have received from other people. Not only do these opportunities benefit us, but they can strengthen relationships with those around us who provided us with the good things we've received.

Today, be sensitive to any feelings you have of entitlement, any sense you have of being deserving of something…and let that feeling go. Simply embrace each moment, accepting things as they are…not as you wish they were or think they should be. Then, when good things happen…which they inevitably will… you can reduce suffering and experience the positive emotions and connection possible when we eliminate the sense of entitlement from our lives.

150

Avoid Complaining

"Thought for the day: Don't tell your problems to people…80% don't care and the other 20% are glad you have them." -Coach Lou Holtz

L ife is not perfect and is certainly not designed to cater to our every whim. Therefore, we all experience things we don't like, things we're unhappy about. When those situations happen, many of us take that opportunity to vent our frustrations to other people. We use our time, and theirs, to describe in detail everything we think is wrong and why. We tell them everything about the situation… what's wrong, why it's wrong, and how other people made it wrong. Each of us is guilty of complaining to others in this way.

We all have also had the misfortune of being the one who is complained to. We've all been forced to sit and listen to someone we care about regale us with the injustices they have incurred, or are incurring, in some facet of their lives. Each of us has had our precious time wasted by a loved one who felt the need to tell us all the things wrong about a particular situation or person.

Consider this question, though. In each scenario, either you complaining to someone else or someone else complaining to you, was anything useful or productive accomplished? Did anything beneficial happen as a result of complaining to someone else? Did anything good come out of listening to someone else complain to you? The answer to both questions is probably a resounding, "No."

When we complain, we accomplish nothing. Identifying problems so solutions can be generated is helpful. Assessing challenges in an effort to affect positive change is a productive and valuable use of time. However, simply complaining about problems does nobody any good at all and is a complete waste of time for both the complainer and the person unlucky enough to be on the receiving end of those complaints.

Today, be on the lookout for complaining. If it's you doing the complaining, stop and replace complaints with possibilities for change. Instead of fixating on what's wrong, focus on what actions might be taken to improve the situation. If it's someone else who's complaining, redirect the conversation to more productive topics. Ask what steps the individual has taken or might take to solve the problem.

Complaining is an entirely pointless and useless activity that should be made extinct in ourselves, in our households, and in our society as quickly as possible. Consider doing your part today to make the extinction of complaining a reality.

151

Big Change Starts Small

"Be the change you wish to see in the world." -Mahatma Gandhi

"Everyone thinks of changing the world, but no one thinks of changing himself." -Leo Tolstoy

Unless you're living in a cave (and if you're reading this, the chances of that are probably low), you are part of a community. In fact, you're probably part of multiple communities. You have friends, family, colleagues, and teammates. You have many different groups you are part of, and those groups can be entangled in complicated ways. That is, your family is also part of your local community, which is part of your state/regional/national/world communities.

Within each of these communities, there are problems. Things aren't perfect. There are policies, habits, attitudes, expectations, and communication styles that you wish were different than they currently are. Because of how big many of these communities are, it can be daunting and overwhelming to think about trying to effect change. So, hoping for things to improve can seem like a complete waste of time.

So, how do things change? Is there anything we can do,

personally, to improve our society? Of course…and it starts at the individual level…with us.

Society is made up of smaller communities which, in turn, are made up of individual people just like you. Change happens when enough individuals decide that things need to be different and then band together to convince others of their point of view. It all begins, however, with us…as individuals…deciding we want things to be different and living the change we want to see.

Taking active steps to convince others our opinions are correct is helpful and useful; however, the most important step is to begin living out the values, attitudes, behaviors, and beliefs we'd like to see in the world. When we do, our kids notice, our spouse notices, our friends and coworkers notice, and our fellow community members notice.

Change begins with us.

Today, live the change you'd like to see. Talking big and selling your ideas is fine. However, it's the example you set that will ultimately convince others and bring their vision for the future in line with yours.

152

Own the Wrongness

"If someone can prove me wrong and show me my mistake in any thought or action, I shall gladly change. I seek the truth, which never harmed anyone: the harm is to persist in one's own self-deception and ignorance." -Marcus Aurelius

At some point today, if it hasn't happened already, you're going to be wrong. It might be a belief you hold or how you interpret someone else's words or actions, but at some point today you will be incorrect.

In those moments, sometimes we're made aware of our wrongness, and sometimes we aren't. Obviously, if we never get information that allows us to correct our views and behavior, then we will go on believing incorrect information and acting on that information as if it were correct. This is unfortunate but unavoidable.

However, we often obtain additional information that makes it clear that our conclusions, and the behaviors that resulted from those conclusions, were wrong. In those situations, it behooves us and everyone around us to adjust our thinking and behavior as quickly as possible. The problem is, though, that those adjustments don't happen as often or as quickly as they should.

When we find out we're wrong, we often get defensive. We perceive being wrong as being the same thing as being inadequate. We take being wrong personally and consider it indicative of some sort of character or personality flaw. We think admitting being wrong is equal to admitting others are better than we are. As a result, since none of us likes feeling inadequate, deficient, or "less than" in any way, we quickly try to rationalize our beliefs and justify why we're right…even when it is abundantly clear that we're wrong.

Today, when that inevitable moment occurs when you realize you're wrong, don't hide it, justify it, fight it, or feel bad about it. Instead, embrace it.

Every time we find out we're wrong, we become better. Every time we gain more accurate information about ourselves, others, or the world than we've had in the past, we gain the ability to make better predictions about our environments and take more productive actions as a result of our new insight.

So, when presented with new, reliable, valid information, change your mind quickly and happily. One of the best gifts we humans have is the ability to think logically and rationally. And the more accurate information we have, the more rationally we can think. So, welcome opportunities to adjust your views and improve your understanding of yourself, those around you, and society at large.

153

Are You Winning?

"Get in the habit of winning at everything." -Geno Auriemma

Maintaining a mindset of trying to "win life" can be helpful…as long as "winning" is defined in the right way.

Typically, winning is defined as doing better at something than someone else. However, winning can be much more broadly defined than this.

For example, we can think of ourselves as "winning" every time we obtain a maximally beneficial outcome. From this viewpoint, we "win" a challenging conversation we have with our child or spouse when the conversation ends with the issue being resolved, both parties satisfied, and the relationship as least as strong as it was before the discussion took place. We "win" at work when we accomplish an objective by interacting with our colleagues in respectful ways that maintain our working relationship and create a comfortable, productive environment. We "win" at restaurants when, while waiting to be seated, we exhibit patience, tolerance, and compassion for the workers who are trying their best to do their jobs as well as they can.

Winning can also be defined not in terms of doing better than someone else but doing better than we, ourselves, have done in the past. From this perspective, if you do better than you did the last time, you win. If you took a test and got a 75 last time and an 80 this time, you win. If the last time you gave a presentation you were panic-stricken and this time you were just a regular brand of nervous, you win. If the last time your child forgot to do something you told them to do you lost your temper and this time you were able to address the situation with regulated emotions and a rationale tone, you win.

Today, broaden your definition of "winning" and adopt a "winning" attitude. Do what you can to win in every situation you encounter. Do what you can to ensure results that are beneficial for you and everybody else involved. Make every effort to do better this time than you did last time.

The more we prioritize winning in these ways, the better off we, our loved ones, and our entire society will be.

154

Commitments and Responsibilities are Living, Too

"You must live in the present, launch yourself on every wave, find your eternity in each moment. Fools stand on their island opportunities and look toward another land. There is no other land, there is no other life but this." -Henry David Thoreau

"One today is worth two tomorrows." -Benjamin Franklin

Most of us can identify with the feeling of being overwhelmed by the number of commitments and responsibilities we have on a daily basis. How those commitments became commitments and whether or not we should have volunteered for all that we have volunteered for are subjects for another time. The salient fact now is that the commitments and responsibilities are here and typically allow for very little downtime. As a result, we often find ourselves thinking about the future, wishing and hoping for the time when our commitments end, so we can take a break…so we can do nothing for a little while.

However, these things we've signed up to do, the responsibilities we've accepted, ARE our lives. They aren't something we do in order to gain access to our lives… they're it. Pining for different circumstances is not helpful, and postponing happiness until some end state is achieved is not productive. Time continues inexorably on, and we have no idea how much of it we have. So, does it make sense to be miserable fulfilling responsibilities in the finite moments of life you're afforded...the moments happening right now...because all of your focus is on some imaginary future moment when you can simply do nothing?

Time is our most precious resource, because it's the one resource we can never, ever replenish. We are given the gift of an unknown, finite amount of time on this planet…with our kids, friends, and loved ones…to share experiences of beauty, joy, love, and meaning.

So, today, strive to embrace those commitments and responsibilities. Remember why you said "yes" to them and keep in mind the good you are capable of doing, not just by completing the commitment, but during every minute you spend fulfilling the commitment. And when the downtime comes, instead of lying inert in front of a television in a vegetative state, use that time to pursue more of the connection, wonder, awe, interest, and engagement this world has to offer.

Think about this, when you're on your deathbed, which will you regret more: time spent doing nothing or time spent on commitments, responsibilities, and other shared experiences with the world?

155

If a Little's Good, More's Better!...Um, No.

"Be moderate in order to taste the joys of life in abundance."
-Epicurus

"Never go to excess, but let moderation be your guide." -Cicero

Over the past decade, the phrase "Go Big, or Go Home" has become ubiquitous in our society. Similar ideals have been expressed as "If a little's good, more's better" and "All or nothing." This idea that nothing is good unless we get as much of it as possible, squeeze every drop out of it we can, permeates our society and creates a number of problems.

For example, many people base their choice of restaurants on which will bring them the largest servings. Restaurants have learned this and supply people, including children, with far more food than they need. It's not hard to find meals on a menu that come close to, if not exceed, the entire recommended daily calorie intake. That is, the total number of calories it takes to run a human body can easily be consumed in one sitting at any mainstream restaurant…and we see this as a good thing.

Similarly, if we want to lose weight, we often reduce our calorie intake to dangerous levels and engage in unsustainable amounts of exercise. Or, we cut out ALL fat (or sugar or carbs or…fill in the blank) from our diets.

And who doesn't know someone incapable of having a conversation that doesn't include some mention of how hard and how many hours they work?

When did we lose the idea of temperance? When did moderation become something no longer valued within our society?

Why can't we simply eat a little bit of everything…protein, carbohydrates, fat, vegetables, dairy, and even sugar? And, why can't we just eat until we're full and then stop?

What if we got a moderate amount of exercise most days and varied our workouts in ways that targeted both strength and cardiovascular improvements?

What if we put in an honest, effortful day at work and then turned our attention toward the other myriad things that make life worth living?

Today, make a list of the categories that matter to you and see if you can do at least something, even if it's small, from each category. Choose relatively healthy food and eat only until you are full, move your body throughout the day, read a book, connect with a family member or loved one, play soccer or a boardgame with your kids, watch a show or movie that you've heard about and have wanted to see, and…yes…go to work and do a great job while you're there.

Life offers a wide variety of experiences, and we can enjoy all of them without taking any one of them to the extreme. Moderation, temperance…a little can go a long way.

156

Why Did I Just Do That?

"We learn the social norms of society and modify our behaviour accordingly."- Jane Goodall

Mores are values and expectations we hold that "go without saying." These rules and norms guide our behaviors every day without us even being aware of their influence. Mores are why students in a classroom will walk in and sit down in a seat, why we form lines when we're with other people trying to obtain the same products or services we are, and why we don't show up to work naked. When we think about it, none of these behaviors is what necessarily HAS to happen. For example, students could walk in and just stand around the walls of the room...or do headstands around the walls of the room for that matter. The order in which people are served could be determined by size and strength, and people could walk around naked whenever and wherever they'd like.

Mores permeate every aspect of our lives. However, most of these norms regularly operate outside of our awareness. We don't even know that our choices are made because they align with implicit rules in our environments. And these mores don't just exist at the societal level. Our work environments, families, athletic teams, and churches all have mores, unwritten rules that govern what is acceptable behavior and what isn't.

What are some of the mores that guide your behavior? Think about the different spheres in which you operate (e.g. social, professional, family, spiritual) and see if you can identify some of the rules that exist in that environment. One way to do this is to tune into your emotions. Notice the times when you feel irritated at someone, embarrassed for someone, or guilty about something you did. Is it because you or another person violated an unwritten norm? Another way to identify mores is to examine your expectations. What do you expect from other people? What do you expect from yourself? For example, do you expect people to be on time, or call if they're going to be late?

The more aware of mores we are, the more tuned in we are to the rules and expectations that influence our behaviors, others' behaviors, and our reactions to others' behaviors. The more cognizant we are of those rules that go without saying, the more we understand others' motivations and the more empathetic, understanding, and compassionate we can be.

157

Recipe for Success

"Success usually comes to those too busy to be looking for it." -Henry David Thoreau

People all around the world, from all walks of life, experience success. Poor/rich people, old/young people, smart/not as smart people, people of color, people with/without college degrees…all sorts of people set and achieve goals regularly. So, since success seems to be available to all categories of people, is success just random? Or, can success be predicted?

It turns out that, despite the wide variation in the types of people who are successful, there are reliable actions and characteristics that allow us to predict the likelihood of people experiencing success. Here are a few examples:

- Rise early
- Work hard
- Accept the reality of your situation
- Stay focused on what you can control

In addition to these basic mental and behavioral factors, attitudes such as the following are critical to success:

- Failure does not exist. If we accomplish our goal, great; if not, we've learned valuable information and grown as a result.
- Change is possible. We are not required to walk the same path we've been walking. Improvement can occur whenever we decide for it to.
- I am capable of being effective. We must always keep in mind our ability to adapt, grow, and advance in both our knowledge and abilities.
- What I do matters. Keeping in mind the value and importance of our goals and actions helps us persevere when faced with setbacks and overcome challenges when they inevitably arise along our path to success.

Success has nothing to do with who you are, where you were born, what color your skin is, or how much money you have. Success comes from deciding every day to adopt attitudes that drive the thoughts and behaviors necessary for daily progress toward whatever goal you've chosen.

158

Why Evil Exists

"Evil does not exist in material nature by itself, but evil exists for every person who understands goodness and who has the freedom of choice between good and bad." -Marcus Aurelius

A question that gets asked, discussed, and thought about a lot is, "Why does evil exist?" The question often comes up in a religious context when people question the existence of a God that is good, but the concept of evil is not only discussed in terms of religion.

Something interesting to think about is the follow-up question, "If evil did not exist, what would exist? What would the world be like?" An answer that seems perfectly reasonable on the surface is, "Good. Without evil, the whole world and everything in it would just be good." However, this answer is fundamentally flawed.

Good cannot exist without evil. Either both are present, or neither is present. The same is true for up/down, left/right, and big/small. These concepts must co-occur or be absent altogether. So, if we want good, then we must accept evil. It doesn't mean that we should either ignore or downplay the importance of evil, nor does the inevitability of evil mean we should feel helpless in its face. On the contrary, accepting evil simply means we honestly acknowledge its existence. In this way, we learn to recognize and identify evil more accurately, so we can deliberately choose good.

Furthermore, the presence of evil does not have to be a bad thing. As mentioned before, evil is the only reason there is such a thing as "good". For example, if everyone in the world held doors open for people, we would never notice when that act of kindness occurred. That action would pass by unnoticed because no alternative behavior existed. As a result, we would experience no appreciation or gratitude when someone held a door open for us. Similarly, we experience a wave of positive emotion any time we win…whatever "winning" might mean in your environment. However, winning can't exist without losing. So, if losing didn't exist… wasn't a possibility at all…winning wouldn't exist either. And neither would the positive emotions that go with it.

All of the feelings and experiences we have that make life meaningful and worth living are only possible if their opposites also exist. And we can only fully appreciate these wonderful feelings and experiences if we have also experienced their less appealing counterparts.

Today, rather than bemoaning the existence of negative emotions, "bad" events, and rude people, use these opportunities to remember and appreciate the times when you've experienced the opposite…the positive emotions, "good" events, and kind people. Recognize that in these moments, you have the choice to succumb to the "evil" or choose "good". You can wallow in and complain about things you don't like or turn your attention toward the aspects of your life, relationships, and situations you do like. The latter will not only be more productive but will reduce suffering as well. So, give it a try today.

159

Heroism is Misunderstood and Overnight Success Is A Fantasy

"Overnight success stories take a long time."- Steve Jobs

"It usually takes more than three weeks to prepare a good impromptu speech. Overnight success is a fallacy. It is preceded by a great deal of preparation. Ask any successful person how they came to this point in their lives, and they will have a story to tell." -Mark Twain

In our culture, stories of people performing amazing, heroic deeds at one critical moment in time and stories of people becoming amazingly rich and/or successful overnight dominate our news cycles and social media feeds…and that fact is extremely unfortunate.

The truth is that the person who hits the buzzer-beating shot, catches the Hail Mary throw, pulls out a clutch presentation under absurd time constraints, or performs emergency first-aid has been preparing for that moment for a very long time. Similarly, the inventor who went from broke to wealthy as the result of a single invention, the actor nobody's heard of who starred in a blockbuster film, and the restauranteur who opened a restaurant chain that seemed to magically appear in every town and city simultaneously have been working for years to achieve their success.

Believing that success and high levels of performance in important moments simply happen automatically, out of nowhere, prevents people from noticing and appreciating the time, effort, sweat, rejection, tears, humility, and perseverance necessary for those moments to occur. ESPN blithely airs footage of amazing, awe-inspiring performances while failing to mention the countless hours of daily practice and preparation athletes engage in daily to ensure they are capable of seizing that opportunity for greatness when it presents itself.

Staying ready is the key, and it's impossible to do if you don't even know it's necessary. We never know when opportunity is going to present itself, but we do know that the key to success is capitalizing on opportunity when it shows up. It is impossible, however, to take advantage of opportunities we aren't ready for.

Today, take steps to stay ready. Put in the work. Stay relentless in your pursuit. Do what's necessary to ensure that you are physically, mentally, emotionally, tactically, technically, socially, and spiritually prepared to recognize and run confidently toward opportunities that cross your path. Then, when your moment arrives, you'll be able to reap the rewards of your "overnight success".

160

Stay Gold

Nature's first green is gold,
Her hardest hue to hold.
Her early leaf's a flower;
But only so an hour.
Then leaf subsides to leaf.
So Eden sank to grief,
So dawn goes down to day.
Nothing gold can stay.

Robert Frost

When was the last time you found yourself insatiably curious about something you encountered? Or, completely and totally engrossed in whatever you were doing or thinking? Or, mesmerized by beauty or complexity that seemed invisible to other people? These are all states kids naturally and frequently experience. However, somewhere along our path to adulthood, our wonder, awe, and curiosity gradually dissipate.

As human beings, we easily become habituated to stimuli in

our environments. That is, when we continually encounter the same things over and over, we tend to take them for granted and even fail to notice them altogether, regardless of what our reactions were when we initially encountered them. This tendency to become accustomed to things quickly and easily saps our joy, limits our growth, and endangers our relationships.

Imagine one of your favorite foods that you don't keep in your house and only come across on an infrequent basis. Now, imagine that same food was readily available to you at all hours of every day. How long would it take for the joy you now experience when eating that food to diminish considerably or even disappear altogether?

Imagine every day was planned out and predictable. From morning to night, you ate basically the same foods, watched the same shows, talked to the same people, went to the same places, and did essentially the same things. For many, imagining this is not hard at all, because it closely approximates the life we already live. Now, think back to when you were first learning to drive. Remember the feelings of nervous excitement and anticipation that went along with even just getting behind the wheel, let alone actually putting the car in "Drive" and pulling into traffic? These new experiences, these opportunities for growth and development, all but disappear once we lose our curiosity and interest in the world.

Imagine your interactions with a friend, spouse, or child…the person who means the most to you in this world. What was the last interaction with this person like? How long did it last? What did you talk about? How much eye contact did you make? Was your full attention devoted to that person, or were you distracted by other thoughts or things going on around you? When our interactions become rote, routine, and repetitive, it's easy to take the other person for granted and lose our appreciation for just what made them such an important part of our lives in the first place.

Make time to recognize and embrace the simple but profound beauty that exists in each moment. Remember the fleeting, ephemeral nature of life and appreciate each moment spent in the company of loved ones. Allow curiosity to wander and explore all aspects of this amazing universe.

And as Johnny so famously told Ponyboy in the classic book/ movie The Outsiders, *"Stay gold."*

161

Now Is When Progress Is Made

"Remember then: there is only one time that is important – Now! It is the most important time because it is the only time when we have any power." -Leo Tolstoy

Failure and lack of progress don't occur because we don't know what we need to do. They occur because we simply don't do what we know we need to do.

Planning can absolutely contribute to the successful completion of a goal, especially a goal that is challenging and complex. However, we can't mistake planning with progress. Generating a route from Point A to Point B using GPS is a very helpful thing to do. However, identifying the route doesn't move us any closer to our ultimate objective. The "Time to Location" provided by the GPS will not change until you actually start moving along the identified path. Progress and success depend on productive action, and that action can only take place in the present moment.

Tomorrow is a wonderful fantasy that many of us cling to regularly. Things will be better tomorrow. I'll be more prepared tomorrow. I'll have more energy or feel better tomorrow. I'll get started tomorrow. The problem with "tomorrow" is that it's not real. It is an illusion that never arrives. If we are going to progress toward a desired goal, that progress will ALWAYS happen in the present moment...right now. So, since we know what we need to do and we know that right now is the only time anything ever actually happens, why not take useful, productive, forward-moving action this very minute.

Today, examine your goals and tune into any tendency you might have to procrastinate, to postpone the actions required to achieve what you'd like to achieve. Remind yourself that this current moment, right now, is not a prelude to anything. It is not like the commercials before a movie or an introduction before a book or the national anthem before a baseball game. This moment is all there is. It IS the movie, the book, and the game. So, use this present moment to do one of the things you know need to be done. Only then will you have made tangible, real progress. Then, because progress feels so good, why not do something else in the next moment? Do that enough times, and success takes care of itself.

162

Just Get Base Hits

"In baseball, my theory is to strive for consistency, not to worry about the numbers. If you dwell on statistics you get shortsighted; if you aim for consistency, the numbers will be there at the end." -Tom Seaver

"The man who moves a mountain begins by carrying away small stones."- Confucious

We live in a homerun culture. Taking big risks to reap big rewards is something we regularly celebrate in our society. Although it's certainly true that the success we notice occasionally follows a "swing for the fence", much more often the success we see and experience results from a series of simple base hits.

A situation we've probably all encountered at some point illustrates this point very well. Think of a time when you came up short. You were competing with someone else and lost by just a little bit. You were up for a promotion at work, but the promotion went to a colleague by a narrow margin. You took a test or wrote a paper in school that you thought was good enough for one grade, but you fell short of your desired grade by only a point or two.

Now, think about why you came up short. What were some things you could have done differently that might have affected the results?

Chances are, the things you thought of weren't big, monumental, earth-shattering changes. Chances are, the things you thought of were small, detail-oriented things that could have been done more frequently, more consistently, and better than you did them before. That is, big, dramatic actions probably didn't come to mind when thinking about what you might have done differently to maximize the likelihood of success. What came to mind were the everyday, mundane activities that are ultimately responsible for success when consistently strung together over a long enough period of time.

If you've been pondering ways to achieve everything you want in one fell swoop, one big swing of the bat, rethink that strategy. Instead, think about what you'd like to achieve and what small steps you can take today, right now, that will move you a little closer to your goal. Focus on the base hit. Focus on incremental progress. Cultivate patience. Become sensitive to, and celebrate more regularly, the steady, reliable headway you make.

Concentrate on, and put your faith in, consistent base hits. If you do, you'll cross the plate and celebrate with your team before you know it.

163

What Is Success?

"What is called genius is the abundance of life and health." -Henry David Thoreau

Many of us rate how well our day went in terms of how busy we were. We remember with pride the number of hours we "did" things. We congratulate ourselves on taking as few breaks as possible. We take great pleasure in detailing to others all the things we've crossed off our "to-do" lists during the day.

In other words, many of us measure the success of our lives in the wrong ways.

Productivity and progress toward goals that are important to you are good things. However, busyness doesn't equal progress, and hectic, chaotic action doesn't equal productivity. So, measuring success in terms of how many hours we kept ourselves running or how many different things we checked off a list is a bad way to measure success. Success should be determined based on the efficiency and effectiveness of our actions. From this standpoint, one person working two hours can be much more productive and progress more than a person working eight hours.

In addition to productivity and progress, however, we can also measure success in terms of the levels of peace, equanimity, and overall well-being we experience throughout the day. The chronic stress and anxiety that often accompanies the continual pursuit of external goals and objectives can be exhausting and can exact a tremendous toll on our physical, psychological, emotional, and social well-being. Learning how to tune into our mental, physical, and emotional states and how to regulate those states effectively can go a long way toward increasing peace and equanimity and decreasing overall suffering.

And here's the kicker…the two different ways of measuring success (productivity/progress and peace/equanimity/well-being) are not mutually exclusive.

That is, if we take time to recognize and feel good about the strategies we've used, effort we've made, attitudes we've adopted, or actions we've taken to make progress…we can enhance our sense of peace and overall well-being. Conversely, if we take time to tune in to and regulate our internal (physical, mental, emotional) state using breathing, meditation, reframing, time with friends/ loved ones…whatever techniques work for us…we set conditions for better productivity and more progress.

How are you measuring success? At the end of the day, what criteria do you use to evaluate how you've used the precious, finite time you were allotted? Do you focus on actual productivity and progress or on busyness? Do you factor in levels of peace, equanimity, and overall well-being when calculating success or just the number of things crossed off your to-do list?

Today, assess how you define success and consider including measures of overall physical, mental, and emotional well-being.

Not only will you feel better, but you will likely notice a boost in productivity and progress as well.

164

The World-Wide Web

"Interbeing is the understanding that nothing exists separately from anything else. We are all interconnected. By taking care of another person, you take care of yourself. By taking care of yourself, you take care of the other person. Happiness and safety are not individual matters. If you suffer, I suffer. If you are not safe, I am not safe. There is no way for me to be truly happy if you are suffering. If you can smile, I can smile too. The understanding of interbeing is very important. It helps us to remove the illusion of loneliness and transform the anger that comes from the feeling of separation." -Thich Nhat Hanh

In the United States, we value independence a great deal. We prioritize self-sufficiency and believe that each person is responsible for their own lot in life. We praise kids for accomplishing goals and working through life's challenges on their own. And we believe we must exhaust all of our personal resources before ever considering asking for help.

Unfortunately, deifying independence in these ways results in our feeling guilty and inadequate when we fail or ask for help. And, of course we would...why wouldn't we? If we were self-sufficient and capable of living independently, we'd be able to succeed without help from anybody else. So, of course we're right to feel personally deficient and like we're burdening others with problems we should be able to solve ourselves.

The truth is…thank goodness…this emphasis on independence, on thriving solely on our own, is misguided and makes no sense given the way the universe actually works.

Physicists and philosophers have accepted for a very, VERY long time that our universe is deterministic. This means that whatever is happening right now is happening because of a series of causes that go back literally to the beginning of time. Obviously, because the universe is incredibly complex and we human beings are incredibly limited, the exact causes of what we experience will always be impossible to fully identify.

The thoughts we have, the emotions we experience, the choices we make, the attitudes and moods we adopt, and everything happening in and around the environments we find ourselves in are all the result of concrete causes we often know very little about and…more importantly…have little to no control over.

This means there is an undeniable, unavoidable connection among all things, human and nonhuman, on this planet and in this universe. We all coexist. Independence is an illusion.

What I do influences my environment, and…at the same time…my environment influences me. Every breath I take in a room with other people affects those people's environments by altering the temperature and number of oxygen and carbon dioxide molecules in the room. Every word I speak and nonverbal message I send affects the thoughts, emotions, and behaviors of other people, and their behaviors and nonverbals, in turn, affect me. All of our present thoughts, feelings, and behaviors were determined by environmental and intrapersonal factors from the past and…at least in part…will determine our thoughts, feelings, and behaviors in the future. So, any decision we make, feeling or thought we have, or physical reaction we experience is caused by myriad other factors joining synergistically in that moment.

The Zen Buddhist master Thich Nhat Hanh often illustrated this fact by pointing out that if you looked deeply enough at a flower, you could see the clouds, rain, sun, air, and even garbage… because it took all of those things to create the conditions that allowed the flower to manifest. In the same way, our thoughts, actions, circumstances, emotions, and decisions all manifest as the result of countless environmental, physical, and interpersonal conditions all coming together in a single moment.

So, today, look more deeply at your life. Look for the existing conditions that allow your energy levels, confidence, motivation, actions, and relationships to manifest in the ways they have. Become aware of and be inspired by the impossibly intricate and inseparable connections that exist among ourselves, other people, and the rest of our environment. Recognize the illusory nature of independence. Humbly acknowledge the fact that nothing we do is done completely on our own.

Then, take this knowledge and awareness out into the world and use it for the benefit of yourself and those around you. Ask for and accept help without feeling inadequate in any way. Provide help to and feel compassion for individuals who find themselves in difficult situations. Draw strength from the interconnectedness of everyone and everything on this planet.

And abolish the misplaced veneration for independence that has so deeply infected our society.

165

Begin Again

"I have not failed. I've just found 10,000 ways that won't work." –
-Thomas Edison

When pursuing a goal, having a plan in place about how to accomplish that goal is definitely useful. Taking the time to identify our goals, some obstacles we need to overcome, and some actions we can take to move ourselves from where we are to where we want to be can absolutely help us move in productive directions.

However, at some point during our goal pursuit Life is going to step in and disrupt our carefully laid plans…and when that happens, those carefully laid plans can actually become our worst enemies.

When Life presents us with unanticipated challenges, an inevitability when pursuing any goal, we can become too attached to the plans we've already developed and committed to. This fixation on the original pathway to success can then close our minds to other viewpoints and strategies that might serve us better given our new circumstances.

When our circumstances change, we need to Begin Again. We need to reassess our situation in light of the new information and reevaluate the plans and strategies we've created when our situation was different. Adopting the mindset of "beginning again" opens us up to possibilities we might easily disregard, overlook, or completely miss altogether if we fail to acknowledge the newness of the situation and stubbornly and rigidly adhere to our previous plans of action.

Today, ask yourself whether you have any plans that might need to be revisited given a change that's occurred. Maybe your child started a new sport, you have a new project at work, your drive time to/from work has increased due to construction on the road, you're in a new relationship, or you have more/fewer resources than you had when you originally set your goal.

If change has occurred, challenge yourself to begin again…to reassess with an open mind how your plan is working and whether adjustments, or even a complete overhaul, need to be made.

There is never only one path to success. And the paths to success that might have worked under one set of circumstances may not work under another. Adopting the attitude and mindset of "Begin Again" helps us think flexibly and remain open to all possibilities. So, choose the path to success that will work for you today…each and every day.

166

The Golden Rule…or the Gold-Plated Rule?

Most of us are familiar with the "Golden Rule": Treat others the way you want to be treated. Like most cliches, the Golden Rule has survived as long as it has, because it has some merit. But what is that merit? What is the outcome that really makes the Golden Rule worth living by?

One outcome that might motivate people to live by the Golden Rule is that people tend to treat us better when we live this way. If we treat others how we'd like to be treated (with patience, respect, honesty, etc), people respond more favorably to us because they feel comfortable around us, trust us, and like us. So, when we choose to live by the Golden Rule, we make it more likely that others will behave in ways we find helpful and pleasurable.

Another outcome that might motivate people to live by the Golden Rule is a reward that comes after death. For example, many of the world's religions teach that we should behave well and strive to help others in order to obtain a better life upon reincarnation (Buddhism), end up on a better world (Hinduism), go to Heaven (Christianity), or get to Paradise (Islam).

However, both of these rationales, treating others well so they'll treat you well or attaining some desired state after death, transform the Golden Rule into the Gold-Plated Rule.

The Golden Rule becomes the Gold-Plated Rule when the main reason we treat others well is that our behavior ultimately benefits us in some way. That is, if it weren't for the benefits I receive …either during this life or after death…as a result of my positive treatment of others, there would be no reason for me to make any effort to treat others well.

What makes the Golden Rule actually golden is when our motivation to treat others well comes from within; when we do the right thing simply because it's the right thing to do; when we treat others well because living out daily our core values of justice, compassion, respect, and equality is an integral part of what makes us who we are.

Today, jettison the Gold-Plated Rule and embrace the Golden Rule. Look for chances to add value and goodness to people's lives. Take advantage of opportunities to help others flourish and thrive. Treat others the way you'd like to be treated, not because of anything they might eventually do for you or some eternal reward but because it's simply the right thing to do.

167

Take the Astronaut-Eye View

"Circling the entire planet in ninety minutes, you see that thin blue arc of the atmosphere. Seeing how fragile the little layer is in which all of humankind exists, you can easily from space see the connection between someone on one side of the planet to someone on the other – and there are no borders evident. So, it appears as just this one common layer that we all exist in." Jeff Ashby – NASA Astronaut

We often fixate totally and completely on ourselves and make decisions as if we were the only people those decisions affect. We perceive ourselves as separate from everything around us, as people who are acting on, and being acted on, by the environment. We behave as though there is a clear separation between ourselves and everything around us. We have *our* jobs, *our* families, *our* friends, *our* cars, *our* problems, *our* possessions, and *our* goals in *our* towns, *our* communities, *our* states, and *our* countries.

However, this separation…this sense of being distinct…is an illusion.

The truth is that we are intimately connected...inextricably linked...to everything around us. We are part of, and inseparable from, everybody and everything in this universe. Every thought we have and emotion we feel is the result of biological factors passed down to us through generations as well as environmental influences that may have occurred as recently as only seconds ago. Every action we take results from a complex combination of present and past factors and affects our environment in ways we can never fully comprehend.

Our universe is a single system of which we are a minute but crucial part. In fact, this system, at least as it currently is, would not exist if we weren't a part of it and playing the roles within it that we currently are. There is no way to understand the universe or anything in it without including ourselves as part of it. Without us, everything would be different.

Consider how connected you are to everything around you. Consider your kids and the fact that they would not exist at all if it weren't for you. Think about your family and friends and how different their lives would be if you weren't a part of them. Have you ever planted a tree, taken care of a pet, or helped someone in any way whatsoever? If so, you have left an indelible mark on the universe, a mark that is uniquely yours.

However, don't limit your consideration to single acts alone. Think about the 2nd, 3rd and 4th order effects of even the smallest things you've done. What good will your child go on to do? What shelter or resources will that tree provide for other animals or people? How much joy will your pet bring to others' lives that would not be possible but for your choice to adopt and care for it?

When we consider the universe and our place in it from this broader vantage point, it's easy to see how every plant, animal, human, mineral...everything that exists, has existed, and will exist…is connected. Thinking about things as separate and distinct makes no sense.

Today, appreciate the unique, complex, awe-inspiring connection that exists among everything in this universe. Take comfort in knowing that, regardless of how challenging your day might become, nothing would be as it is without you being a part of it… exactly as you are.

168

Let the Small Fires Burn

"Beware lest you lose the substance by grasping the shadow." -Aesop

With the everyday busyness most of us experience daily, it's easy to get caught up in the minutia of the world. We bounce haphazardly from one thing to the next, our attention being yanked back and forth by the myriad forces competing for it at any given moment. If we're not careful, we can find ourselves going from morning to night simply reacting to situation after situation, putting out one fire after another, with no thought at all directed toward how our actions fit into a larger, overall plan.

Two strategies can help avoid this pinball-like existence: 1) Pause at least every hour to assess whether what you're doing is aligned with your overall objectives and 2) Pause briefly between tasks or activities to fully shift your mind from what you were doing to what you are about to do.

Having a set time to check in with ourselves about our day can help us avoid the unproductive trips down the rabbit holes of life's inevitable unpredictabilities. Although we can't control when unanticipated challenges will arise, we can absolutely control the extent to which we allow these situations to consume our time and attention. It's very easy to get sucked into these attentional maelstroms, but with regular, periodic check-ins, we can ensure that we don't get dragged too far underwater before resurfacing and recommencing our journey along our desired azimuth.

Deliberately pausing between tasks and activities is helpful as well. We can only pay attention to one thing at a time, so our attentional efficiency and effectiveness depends almost exclusively on how well we can shift and sustain attention. We maximize our attentional efficiency when we accept that it takes our brains a little while to transition from one task or situation to another and intentionally take a moment to let go of What Was and move to What Is.

Today, use these strategies to minimize potential distractions, focus on the most important thing in a given moment, and ensure that you're spending your valuable, finite time in ways aligned best with your overall goals and objectives.

169

Just Stop Digging

"If you find yourself in a hole, stop digging." -Will Rogers

As should certainly come as no shock, sometimes things in life don't go how we want them to. This occurrence is ubiquitous, unavoidable, and something each of us encounters all too regularly. However, what comes next tends to vary a great deal…from person to person and situation to situation.

When things go wrong, there are really only three different ways we can act: 1) Get upset and complain, 2) Get discouraged and quit, or 3) Accept what's happened and adapt.

The first two possible responses to adversity are equivalent to continuing to dig after finding ourselves in a hole. Getting angry, blaming others, and complaining to anybody who will listen cause suffering for ourselves and those around us and get us absolutely no closer to solving whatever problem we've encountered. Similarly, allowing ourselves to feel helpless and defeated creates a sense of hopelessness that prevents us from taking any steps at all toward alleviating whatever issues we're facing.

Instead, we need to accept what's happened, evaluate our situation, create a plan to deal with our circumstances, and then ACT! Acceptance, in this case, is not the same as resignation. Acceptance simply means that we have a thorough, honest, and accurate understanding of what's going on and have acknowledged that reality for what it is. Once we've done this, we can evaluate the various options available to us and develop a strategy that leverages the options we can control. Finally, we act on that plan. Chances are, we won't be able to enact all facets of the plan all at once or eliminate our problems in one fell swoop. What we CAN do, however, is act on the first step of our plan...and once that's complete act on the next step, and then the next.

Life presents us with no shortage of challenges...holes we find ourselves in. However, whether we make the hole even deeper (discouragement/quitting/anger/vengeance) or climb out is entirely up to us.

170

"Sorry" Is Not A Bad Word

"Never ruin an apology with an excuse." -Benjamin Franklin

No one among us lives a perfect life. None of us treat everybody with kindness, dignity, and respect all the time. We all make mistakes. Most of us cause others some level of suffering at some point...sometimes at multiple points...every day. When we behave in these ways, when we recognize that we have done something we shouldn't have done, something that has hurt someone else physical, mentally, or emotionally, we can react in one of two ways: 1) Justify to ourselves and others why we did what we did or 2) Accept responsibility and apologize for our mistake.

Our natural tendency as human beings is to justify our behavior. We tend to argue vehemently for the rationality and normality of our choices, even though our choices may clearly contradict values and priorities we purport to hold. For example, after losing our temper and snapping at a child, spouse, or colleague, we might justify that behavior we know to be wrong by pointing out our hunger, blaming our lack of sleep, or faulting some choice or personality characteristic of the other individual. Reacting in this way reduces what's known as cognitive dissonance, the unpleasant feeling we get when the way we think we should behave doesn't match the way we actually behave. However, it doesn't help our situation. Failing to acknowledge our own shortcomings dooms us to repeat the same mistakes, and blaming others for our own iniquities corrodes and will ultimately destroy our relationships.

Instead of ego protection, we need humility. Instead of blaming, we need to accept responsibility. Instead of figuring out how to excuse our mistakes, we need to acknowledge and apologize for those mistakes. Only in this way can we foster growth and learning for ourselves and strengthen and develop our relationships with others.

Today, when you do or say something you probably shouldn't have, pay attention to how you respond. Do you readily acknowledge the mistake and immediately try to make amends, or do you search for reasons why your behavior is acceptable...or at least understandable? In these unpleasant but unavoidable moments in life, challenge yourself to humbly accept responsibility for your actions and ask forgiveness from the person you've harmed. Suffering will decrease, your relationship will strengthen, and the lessons you take away will make you both happier and wiser.

171

Forgive and Remember

"How can you say to your brother, 'Let me take the speck out of your eye,' when all the time there is a plank in your own eye? You hypocrite, first take the plank out of your own eye, and then you will see clearly to remove the speck from your brother's eye." Matthew 7: 4-5

People harm other people. It's part of life. Much more frequently than we'd like, we are treated by others in ways we believe are wrong. When this occurs, we are quick to feel anger, frustration, and resentment and often respond by lashing out at the other person or withdrawing, while we allow our minds to seethe and ruminate about the wrong we believe has been committed. We experience intense negative emotions and turn our attention to what sort of punishment we will exact on the individual who has dared harm us in so blatant and inconsiderate a manner.

Being harmed by others is unavoidable, but suffering as a result of that harm is not. In these situations, four actions will quickly relieve our suffering and move us back onto a path of productivity.

First, we need to question our assumption that the person has harmed us intentionally or because of some inherent character flaw. We need to remember all of the occasions…and we usually don't have to go too far back in time…when we've made mistakes, when we've spoken or acted in ways that were insensitive or harmful to others. Once we realize that we've been on the other side of the situation more times than we'd like to admit, we can better demonstrate both compassion and forgiveness.

Second, we need to realize that nobody makes us feel anything. Our emotions result from our perceptions, the meaning we assign to what happens in our world, and we are entirely responsible for those perceptions. We can choose to focus on whatever aspect of our circumstances we'd like and interpret things in whatever way is best for us and those we care about. So, after questioning our assumptions about the other person's intent, we need to accept responsibility for our own emotional reaction to their behavior by becoming aware of the ways in which our perceptions and interpretations…the ways in which we are choosing to view the situation…are causing us suffering in this moment.

Third, we need to forgive the other person. Forgiveness doesn't mean endorsing what the other person did or communicating in any way that their words or actions were appropriate or acceptable. Forgiveness simply means letting go of our own anger and resentment. It means letting go of the past and focusing on the present, what can be done right now to deal with circumstances as they are.

Lastly, we need to remember what has happened. At first glance, this seems the exact opposite of "letting go of the past." However, there is a difference between accepting and moving on from what was and forgetting completely about what was. Valuable lessons can and should be learned from our past experiences. Therefore, we need to remember what has occurred, so we can avoid the same issue, or deal more effectively with the issue, in the future.

Try these four things the next time someone does something harmful to you. You might be surprised at how quickly your suffering is eliminated, and your relationships with others are clarified, restored, and possibly even strengthened through the power of awareness, acceptance, compassion, and forgiveness.

172

Make a Plan

"It takes as much energy to wish as it does to plan." -Eleanor Roosevelt

"By failing to prepare, you are preparing to fail." -Benjamin Franklin

L ife is busy. We have families, jobs, hobbies, friends…and they all have one thing in common. They require time. Time to drive to/from houses, offices, and soccer fields. Time to shop for and cook meals. Time to share our experiences, accomplishments, hopes, and fears with our loved ones.

All of the things that make life worth living involve the use of this essential resource called time, but time is both finite and unrenewable. It is the only resource we have access to that we can never get more of. We are allotted the amount of time we are, and that's it. So, it is imperative that we value time and use time as wisely and conscientiously as possible.

And one way of doing that is by making plans.

Although they can be time-consuming and easily affected by unforeseen circumstances, plans are the best ways to make sure we are aware of all the things we need to do, prioritize the most important of those things, and track progress on a regular basis.

First, plans allow us to offload from your mind much of what may be causing us angst. There is power in writing down all of the obligations and responsibilities swirling around in our heads. Putting these down on "paper" (technology is fine, too) frees our minds to focus on accomplishing our tasks rather than remembering what those tasks are.

Next, once our plans are down on paper, it's much easier to glance through our lists and mark the most important things. Prioritizing your tasks can help ensure we get the biggest bang for our effort and energy bucks. With so many responsibilities spread across so many different facets of life, it's very easy to lose sight of what's most important. However, simply starring the items that we absolutely need to do helps direct our attention to that most important thing and makes it more likely that we will get done what we really need to get done.

Finally, plans allow us to track our progress reliably. Clearly and regularly seeing progress limits the amount of time spent wondering if we've forgotten anything and provides a feeling of improvement and success each time a task on the list gets completed. Although seemingly small, the joy associated with marking something as Complete should not be overlooked.

What's your plan for today…or tomorrow? Some people make plans the night before and some the morning of. Which time is better depends on which one you will actually commit to doing.

Remember, too, that making a plan doesn't guarantee the plan will work exactly as you envisioned it. However, even if Life steps in with unexpected challenges, having a plan clarifies your priorities for the day. With this knowledge, you can make better decisions about any adjustments required for what you've deemed truly important.

173

Focus on the Stuff You'll Remember

"It is good to have an end to journey toward; but it is the journey that matters, in the end."- Ernest Hemingway

Pursuing goals involves at least two different paradoxes.

Paradox 1: We obviously need to know what our goal is if we're going to achieve it, but achieving our goal requires us to forget our goal…at least most of the time.

Before we can achieve a goal, we need to identify, very clearly and specifically, what that goal is. We need to determine exactly what our desired outcome looks like and by when that outcome should be achieved. Then, we need to create a plan, a step-by-step process we can follow that will lead us to our ultimate objective. During both of these first two aspects of goalsetting, our attention must necessarily focus on the goal we've identified.

However, in order to actually achieve our goal, we need to focus not on the goal itself but on the things that will help us achieve that goal. We need to turn our attention away from the desired outcome and toward the thoughts, emotions, and actions that will ultimately lead to success.

Paradox 2: We set goals because of the benefits we believe we'll receive once we reach our desired end states, but the biggest benefits of goalsetting come not from the achievement of the goal but from the pursuit of the goal.

Because of human beings' natural inclination toward homeostasis, the joy, pride, and sense of accomplishment we feel after achieving a goal quickly disappear. These positive emotions might last for a few days or even a few weeks, but they are remarkably short-lived. This is why we find ourselves…almost immediately upon completion of one goal…asking, "What's next?" So, achieving our goals has some benefits for sure; however, the primary benefits we receive from goals come from the goal pursuit process itself.

While pursuing our goals, we learn and improve a variety of skills, enhance and strengthen relationships, develop wisdom, and create memories we tell stories about for years. And, unlike the positive emotions associated with goal achievement, these benefits remain with us for the rest of our lives.

Think about goals you've achieved in the past…what do you remember most vividly? Is it the ultimate achievement of the goal or the pursuit of the goal…what you endured and overcame to attain your objective?

Goals are achieved little by little, step by step, in the here and now. Today, put your attention on what's happening in the present moment. Focus on the attitudes and behaviors necessary to get you from where you are to where you want to be…and enjoy the process itself!

174

Why Is Impermanence Good?

Shed no tear – O, shed no tear!
The flower will bloom another year.
Weep no more – O, weep no more!
Young buds sleep in the root's white core.
John Keats

"Thanks to impermanence, everything is possible." -Thich Naht Hanh

Impermanence refers to the fact that the universe...including us...is constantly changing. As a result, nothing is the same from day to day, hour to hour, minute to minute, or second to second.

As real and inevitable as impermanence is, though, it can be a difficult concept for we human beings to accept. So, we create the illusion that it doesn't exist. We do our best to construct steady, predictable environments in which our habits are easily maintained (for better or worse), our assumptions are accurate most of the time, and our security and stability are preserved.

Living in this illusory world, however, prevents us from fully realizing at least four benefits that go along with recognizing, appreciating, and embracing impermanence:

1. *Relationships improve.* When we realize that nothing is permanent, not even our relationships with those closest to us, we wake up to the importance of the little things. We are more apt to make time for our loved ones, give our loved ones our full and undivided attention, and treat our loved ones with more patience and compassion.

2. *Gratitude experiences become more genuine and more frequent.* When we truly understand that our circumstances will inevitably change, we become more sensitive to the gifts that we have in the present moment and are quicker to appreciate the things, people, and circumstances in our lives that provide comfort and generate positive emotion.

3. *Acceptance of our true reality becomes easier.* When we fully embrace the concept of impermanence, we shed the illusion that everything will stay the same and no longer fear change. On the contrary, we recognize that change is not only unavoidable but desirable. Acceptance allows us to view our current situation not just in terms of how it is but how it could be…which leads us to….

4. *Hope is possible.* Impermanence creates the potential for growth, development, and improvement. When we acknowledge and accept impermanence, we open ourselves up to an infinite number of possibilities for thriving that would otherwise be unimaginable.

Where do you see impermanence in your life? How might you use the concept of impermanence to build your relationships, improve your gratitude, accept your reality, and generate hope?

How might embracing the impermanence in every facet of your life set you on a pathway to flourishing that you'd never thought existed?

175

Habits...Should We Make Them or Break Them?

"A child-like man is not a man whose development has been arrested; on the contrary, he is a man who has given himself a chance of continuing to develop long after most adults have muffled themselves in the cocoon of middle-aged habit and convention." -Aldous Huxley

"Make a habit of two things: to help, or at least to do no harm." -Hippocrates

As human beings, we are creatures of habit. We are hardwired to develop patterns of thinking, feeling, and acting that are stable, consistent, and predictable. Sometimes this is a good thing, and sometimes it isn't.

When most of us think of habits, we think of bad habits... smoking, drinking, biting fingernails, or eating dessert before bed. These bad habits are ones that we readily recognize as being unhelpful at best and harmful at worst. Whether we do anything to actually eliminate these habits is a different story, but most of us can get on board with the notion that not having these habits would be better than having them.

However, habit formation involves much more than the prototypical counterproductive habits described above. Our behaviors when we wake up, routes we regularly drive, and initial thoughts and reactions to things that happen (e.g., baby crying, phone buzzing, people being late) are all examples of habits that form through the daily living out of our lives. And those habits can be helpful or not.

Habits can be productive or counterproductive for several reasons. Habits are productive when they help us automate healthy thoughts, emotions, and behaviors. For example, if I develop the habit of reflecting on at least three things I'm grateful for before I go to sleep and immediately upon waking up, this habit can generate the positive emotion of gratitude and have wonderful benefits on my physical, psychological, emotional, and social well-being. Similarly, the habit of putting workout clothes on the end table next to the bed before I go to sleep and immediately donning those clothes as soon as I wake up can help ensure my body gets the necessary amount of regular physical activity it needs.

Habits are counterproductive when they automate thoughts, attitudes, and behaviors that are unhealthy or stifle our natural curiosity and creativity. Smoking, drinking alcohol, and eating ice cream before bed are all examples of counterproductive behaviors that can become automatic and almost unconscious all too easily. Likewise, a thought of, "Here we go again" every time we walk in the door to work is counterproductive in that the thought likely drives counterproductive emotions (e.g., irritation), attitudes (e.g., "let's get this over with"), and behaviors (e.g., simply doing the minimum necessary not to get fired) that quickly become automatic as well.

Habits are counterproductive, too, when they stifle creativity and curiosity. When our perspectives and ways of engaging with the world are calcified by habit, we are less likely to notice things we've never noticed before, generate novel ideas and solutions, and fully experience the incredible abundance and nuance within our environments.

So, should we make or break habits? Yes. We should do both.

Today, examine the habits that already exist in your life and determine whether those habits are productive or counterproductive. Remember that thoughts, attitudes, and emotions can become habits the same way actions become habits. If your habits are productive, great! Keep them. If they are counterproductive, replace your counterproductive thoughts, attitudes, or actions with more productive ones and deliberately, intentionally, and regularly practice those new habits every day.

Next, evaluate your values and goals and ask yourself what one new habit would help you live out your values more consistently or achieve your goals more quickly. Then, with intentionality, initiate that habit and check in regularly to see how consistent you are with its implementation.

176

We Always Have At Least One Choice

"Everything can be taken from man but one thing: the last of the human freedoms, to choose one's attitude in any given set of circumstances."- Viktor Frankl

"Some things are within our power, while others are not. Within our power are opinion, motivation, desire, aversion, and, in a word, whatever is of our own doing; not within our power are our body, our property, reputation, office, and, in a word, whatever is not of our own doing." -Epictetus

In the hectic, tumultuous world in which we live, it is easy to feel overwhelmed by the sheer volume of things we juggle daily. Our jobs, families, friends, chores, and other responsibilities are constantly present and often challenge us in ways that put the water right at our chins. In these situations, we can feel completely helpless and at the mercy of the world around us.

Although difficult for many of us to accept, the truth is that we have little to no control over the vast majority of our lives.

Everything is impermanent and in a constant state of flux, including ourselves, and the reality is that we can control nothing except…as Epictetus put it, "…whatever is of our own doing."

As Frankl pointed out, however, one of those things that is "of our own doing"…that we can always control…is our attitude. What we choose to focus on, the importance we place on certain events, the ways that we perceive and explain what happen to us… all of that is in our control and can never be taken away.

Although adopting attitudes that shield us from hopelessness and restore our equanimity amid the chaos of our everyday existence is simple, it's not easy. Altering our attitudes is simple in that it requires only that we switch our focus from one thing to another, that we change our counterproductive way of viewing and understanding our situation to a more productive way of seeing and understanding what is going on in our lives. Altering our attitudes is not easy, though, because in the actual moment of crisis, our fight-or-flight mode (sympathetic nervous system) has been activated.

To help us grab control of our thoughts and attitudes in those moments when we are overcome with feelings of helplessness and hopelessness, it helps to identify and practice adopting helpful, productive thoughts during our more peaceful moments. While in the eye of the storm, bring to mind 3-4 core values you hold (e.g., courage, patience, compassion). Then, create an image associated with each of these values, an image that evokes powerful feelings associated with each value. Next, regularly practice bringing that image to mind, ensuring that you feel the strong emotions that go with that image. Finally, when you find yourself in a challenging, stressful situation, bring to mind that image and experience those emotions. This will immediately restore a sense of control and equanimity.

With the restored sense of control, you are now able to reassess and reappraise the situation. How accurate is your current assessment of what's going on? Is there another way to view what's happening that is more productive? For example, is there any potential goodness that can come out of your current circumstances? How might you grow from the experience you're having? Is it possible to be grateful that things aren't worse than they are?

Chaotic, stressful situations are impossible for us to avoid. However, by reminding ourselves of what's really important to us…the values we hold most dear…we can adopt attitudes aligned with those values and immediately experience a sense of control and equanimity, even while surfing the hurricane waves of life.

177

Your Best Self

"Do the best you can until you know better. Then, when you know better, do better." - Maya Angelou

"How noble and good everyone could be if, every evening before falling asleep, they were to recall to their minds the events of the whole day and consider exactly what has been good and bad. Then without realizing it, you try to improve yourself at the start of each new day."
-Anne Frank

All of us have good days and bad days. We have some days when we are proud of our actions, attitudes, and words, and we have other days we'd rather pretend never happened. Living life as our "best selves" is a challenging thing to pull off, especially on a consistent, daily basis. It's even harder, though, when we're not clear on what our "best self" even looks like. How do we know when our "best selves" are what we're bringing to the world?

Answering this question begins with defining your "best self". What is it? Here are some questions that can help us recognize when our "best self" is on display for the world.

When I am my "best self":

1. What values do I embody? If patience is something I value, do I demonstrate that patience by keeping my cool and remaining calm in situations that otherwise might cause stress and angst?

2. Who am I with? Am I with people who truly matter to me, who make me a better person by bringing out the best in me?

3. What am I doing with my time? Are my pursuits aligned with my values? Am I engaged in activities that are ultimately productive and helpful for me and those I care about?

4. How do I deal with adversity? When unexpected challenges arise, do I handle them with wisdom, poise, and equanimity?

5. How do I interact with others? Do I treat others with respect and grace? Do I demonstrate kindness, compassion, and forgiveness?

Being at our best every moment of every day is impossible. However, the clearer we are about what our "best selves" look like, the more quickly we recognize when our thoughts, speech, and actions in a given moment don't represent the person we truly are at our core.

Today, define your "best self". What are you like, who are you with, what are you doing, and how are acting when you feel most truly and authentically yourself? With this picture in mind, check in with yourself throughout the day. Notice what aspects of your thoughts, attitudes, behaviors, and words reflect your "best self" and which don't. Then adjust.

178

Where Does Wisdom Come From?

"We can understand wisdom in three ways: first, by meditation; this is the most noble way. Secondly, by being influenced by someone or following someone; this is the easiest way. Third is the way of experience; this is the most difficult way." -Confucius

Wisdom is one of the four cardinal virtues (along with Courage, Temperance, and Justice) and has been sought and valued for millennia. But, what is wisdom?

Quite often, wisdom and knowledge are conflated, but the two are actually very different things. Irish rugby player Brian O' Driscoll put the difference between knowledge and wisdom best when he said, "Knowledge is knowing that a tomato is a fruit; wisdom is knowing not to put it in a fruit salad."

Wisdom is clearly valuable and helpful in many ways…but how do we get it?

As mentioned in the quote above, Confucius believed that

wisdom can be acquired in three different ways: meditation, learning from others, and experience.

Gaining wisdom through meditation occurs because of the increased awareness we gain while meditating. Meditation opens us up to a wealth of knowledge about our thoughts and behavior patterns that typically lie under the surface of our awareness. With this knowledge, we gain valuable insight into ourselves through the relationships we discern among these patterns of thoughts and behaviors. Awareness of these connections then facilitates better judgments and decisions…wisdom.

Wisdom can also be gained by learning from other people. We have the benefit not only of learning from the many people around us every day, but from the plethora of brilliant, innovative people who have lived throughout time. Expanding our learning beyond our own small bubbles of existence, throughout time and history, enables us to encounter and absorb vast amounts of information we would otherwise never have become aware of and make connections and come to realizations that would not otherwise have been possible.

Finally, we gain wisdom through our own unique experiences. Everything that makes its way into our consciousness provides useful information about ourselves, others, and the world around us. Through our own personal experiences, we test hypotheses about how the universe operates, gaining knowledge that leads to revelatory insights we experience at a visceral level and can translate into more accurate conclusions and better judgments.

How will you pursue wisdom today? Will you seek greater clarity and insight into yourself and your environment through meditation, by learning from other people, or by fully and intentionally immersing yourself in your experiences?

Or maybe give all three a try….

179

Don't Mistake the Means for the End: Knowledge and Wisdom

"Knowledge comes; but wisdom lingers."- Alfred Lord Tennyson

Knowledge is important. However, gaining knowledge is simply one strategy we use for achieving a desired end state…not an end state in and of itself.

Learning can be an exciting and fun thing to do. Whether we're getting more information about interesting historical figures, improving our understanding of mathematics, or developing proficiency with some sort of physical activity, adding to our knowledge base can be an enjoyable process. But none of that is the point of knowledge.

So, what is the point? What is the ultimate end state obtaining knowledge allows us to achieve?

Obtaining knowledge allows us to develop wisdom.

Each new fact we learn adds one more piece to the puzzle

of our universe. Every new piece of information, when joined with the other pieces of information we've acquired over the years, facilitates a more accurate and thorough understanding of ourselves, others, and the world around us. This continually expanding and increasingly complex web of knowledge allows us to consider our circumstances from more complicated and nuanced angles. And all of this increases our ability to comprehend our thoughts, actions, and environments at deeper and deeper levels, enhancing our wisdom every step of the way. So, the point of gaining knowledge isn't to impress ourselves or others with how many facts we know or skills we have. The point of knowledge is to cultivate a profound, nuanced understanding of our universe that facilitates better, wiser decisions beneficial for ourselves and those around us.

Today, make an effort to learn something new, gain a more in-depth understanding of something you've already learned, or improve your proficiency at a particular skill...but don't stop there. Ask yourself, too, how your enhanced knowledge and new skill set fit in with and connect to other information and experiences, help you more accurately and thoroughly understand your environment, and facilitate better interactions with others. In this way, you can move closer to the ultimate end state of wisdom.

180

Don't Mistake the Means for the End: Rules and Connection/ Cooperation

"Chieftains must understand that the spirit of the law is greater than its letter." -Attila the Hun

Rules and laws can certainly be helpful. However, rule compliance is simply a strategy for achieving an objective… not the objective itself.

Rules in our society can be comforting. Whether they're explicitly defined rules or unwritten social mores, shared and agreed-upon boundaries and expectations provide us with structure and predictability in a volatile and uncertain world. But that's not the real point of rules and laws.

So, what is the point? What is the ultimate objective rules and laws allow us to achieve?

Rules foster connection and cooperation.

In the United States, we like to tout the importance of independence. However, the truth is that independence is an illusion. We are not single individuals drawing solely on personal resources to make our own ways in the world. Instead, we are all members of one very intricately connected global system. Our behaviors affect others, and others' behaviors affect us. Rules and laws help us work and live together within this system in ways that are mutually beneficial for everybody.

So, the point of rules and laws isn't to dictate or limit our behaviors by prescribing mindless compliance with whatever the rule/law states. It's not the letter of the rule or law that matters. What's important is that we understand the intent of the rules/laws... why they were created, how they contribute to an environment of cooperation, and the ways in which they foster connection within a strong, smoothly functioning community.

Today, notice the rules and laws that you follow. Recognize both the explicitly written rules (e.g., traffic laws) and the unwritten rules (e.g., not interrupting when someone is speaking) that guide our daily choices and interactions...but don't stop there. Explore, too, the intent of the rule/law. Why was it created? What value was it designed to uphold? What situation was it created to prevent? And...why are those things important? Why does it matter that the value is upheld or situation is prevented? How does meeting the intent of the rule/law help us develop cohesion and connection with others, enhance cooperation with those around us, and benefit society as a whole?

Answers to these questions help us live the spirit of the law and avoid getting fixated on the individual trees of compliance while missing the forest of intent.

181

Celebrate Others' Stupidity

"Holding onto anger is like grasping a hot coal with the intent of throwing it at someone else. You are the one who gets burned."
-Gautama Buddha

"When you wake up in the morning, tell yourself: The people I deal with today will be meddling, ungrateful, arrogant, dishonest, jealous and surly. They are like this because they cannot tell good from evil. But I have seen the beauty of good, and the ugliness of evil, and have recognized that the wrongdoer has a nature related to my own - not of the same blood or birth, but the same mind, and possessing a share of the divine. And so none of them can hurt me. No one can implicate me in ugliness. Nor can I feel angry at my relative, or hate him. We were born to work together like feet, hands and eyes, like the two rows of teeth, upper and lower. To obstruct each other is unnatural. To feel anger at someone, to turn your back on him: these are obstructions." Marcus Aurelius

Unless fully sequestered for 24-hour periods, we will inevitably encounter people and situations that baffle, disappoint, irritate, or outright enrage us every day. Whether it's the person in the left lane driving the same speed as the person in the right lane, the person writing a check or searching for exact change in line at the grocery store, or the customer support agent with no knowledge related to your problem other than what is contained in the script on their computer, we regularly encounter people and circumstances that challenge our peace and equanimity.

The bad news is that annoying people have existed since people first came into being and will continue to exist until people are extinct. The good news is that there are very effective strategies for dealing with these people that Stoics, Buddhists, and modern-day psychologists agree are extremely helpful.

Acceptance – The first thing we need to do is to accept reality as it is. As Marcus Aurelius points out in the quote above, annoying, evil, dull-witted people walk the Earth right along with the rest of us, and that's simply a fact we need to acknowledge and come to grips with.

Recognize Connectedness – "Interbeing" is a term used frequently by Thich Naht Hanh to describe the symbiotic, synergistic nature of everything in our universe, the idea that we are so intricately interconnected with everything around us that separation is impossible. This concept is one echoed by Marcus Aurelius in the quote above and when he said:

"Frequently consider the connection of all things in the universe and their relation to one another. For in a manner all things are implicated with one another, and all in this way are friendly to one another; for one thing comes in order after another, and this is by virtue of the active movement and mutual conspiration and the unity of the substance."

Accept Responsibility – We are responsible for our thoughts and the ways we perceive the situations around us. As Epictetus reminds us, "It's not things that upset us; it's our judgment about things." If we are experiencing negative emotions, it is the result of how we choose to view the situation we're in. So, how do we view these incredibly annoying people in ways that foster positive instead of negative emotions? Remember that we can be annoying, too.

Choose Humility – We must remember that we are not perfect. We make mistakes and are not immune from behaving in callous, irresponsible, inconsiderate ways. As Marcus Aurelius urges, *"When you are annoyed at someone else's mistake, immediately look at yourself and reflect how you also fail."*

Be Grateful for the Opportunity to Grow – Fortitude, patience, and compassion are valuable qualities that benefit us and those around us. However, these qualities don't just arise; they are developed and improved through practice. So, how can we practice enduring challenges, subduing impulses, and empathizing with others? We put ourselves in situations that require these skills to be used. Every interaction with an annoying person allows us to practice using every one of these skills. Therefore, we should be grateful to these individuals who unknowingly but fortuitously provide us with ample opportunity for self-improvement.

The bottom line is that we will never escape people who act in ways that we believe they shouldn't. However, we can escape the negative emotions often associated with these people's behaviors. Today, notice your physical, mental, emotional, and behavioral reactions when people's actions go against your desires or your beliefs about what "should" be. Then, take the steps described above to not only endure the situation, but benefit from the situation.

182

Perseverance is Great…Until It Isn't

"Never give in. Never, never, never, never – in nothing, great or small, large or petty. Never give in except to convictions of honor and good sense." -Winston Churchill

Perseverance is a valuable characteristic and benefits us in many ways. However, there is a fine line between perseverance and stubbornness.

When discussing virtues, Aristotle introduced the "Golden Mean," a concept grounded in the notion of moderation. According to Aristotle, virtues exist in the middle of a continuum anchored at either end by a vice. For example, courage can be thought of as existing on a continuum between the two vices of recklessness at one end and cowardice at the other.

Through this lens, perseverance can be thought of as existing on a continuum between the two vices of stubbornness and acquiescence. It's bad to give in easily to challenges and pressures, but it's equally bad to continue trying to accomplish something that is simply not possible...at least at the moment. Nothing will ever be achieved if we give up immediately; however, we waste valuable time, energy, and sanity when we continue forcing a square peg in a round hole. Somewhere in the middle lies the sweet spot of perseverance.

The next time you find yourself in a challenging situation, wondering if you should continue or quit, ask yourself where you are on the perseverance continuum. Are you acquiescing... giving up too soon without giving success a fair chance? Are you stubbornly banging your head against the proverbial wall with little chance of a payoff worth the energy and effort you're expending? Or, are you existing within and operating from within the "Golden Mean" of perseverance?

183

Make the Right Choice

"A good decision is based on knowledge, not on numbers." -Plato

With the speed at which life moves and challenges arise, it can be difficult to feel confident about all of the decisions we make. Often, we fall into the trap of believing we don't have time to adequately process the voluminous amounts of information with which we are continually bombarded. This belief leads us to make rash, impulsive decisions that are little more than rolls of the dice.

The truth is, however, that we have plenty of time to process our situations if we cultivate two essential resources: Acceptance and Self-Awareness.

Acceptance allows us to embrace the reality with which we are faced. Rather than wishing things were different, hoping things will change, or outright ignoring what we find unpleasant, we honestly acknowledge the raw truth of our circumstances. Once we accept the present moment as it is, we can critically assess our situation and devise the best courses of action.

Self-awareness allows us to honestly identify our strengths and weaknesses, both in general and during specific moments, and use this knowledge to guide our choices. For example, the drive and commitment to finish what we start is a strength in most situations. However, when presented with a plate overflowing with enough food to feed a small village, feeling compelled to finish the meal we begin is a weakness. Similarly, the ability to think in creative, outside-the-box ways is generally a strength. However, spending time and effort trying to devise a new way to do something for which an efficient and effective protocol already exists is not the best use of our resources.

When we fully and honestly accept our current circumstances as they truly are and maintain an awareness of our strengths and weaknesses, we are better able to make wise, sound judgments in an efficient and timely manner.

The next time you feel overwhelmed by events but have important decisions that need to be made, pause briefly and take a few intentional breaths. During those few seconds, truly accept the reality of your circumstances and utilize self-awareness. You will gain clarity about both the true nature of your situation and the personal resources you can leverage in that moment. Options come to mind more easily, and decisions are made more confidently. Stress levels drop, and well-being rises. And all of this enables you to flourish and thrive in this fast-paced circus we call life.

Made in the USA
Las Vegas, NV
04 October 2023

78532174R00233